What People Are

*Google AdWords Insider*

"I was lucky enough to be one of Simon Leung's first apprentices, and he has **taught me so much** and **brought me so much success** that I am now Simon's business partner for our AdWords and Internet Marketing outsourcing services. Thanks to Simon, I am also now an International speaker, teaching others what he has taught me over the years.

Not only did Simon develop the AdWords optimization strategies at Google, but he's now **training our outsourcing team** the exact same strategies, many of them Simon shares in *Google AdWords Insider* – which is a must read if you want to take your online b

- Andy Huang, Co-
www.AimVenture.c

"I've studied all the Internet Marketing Let me tell you, there's a **new sheriff in AdWords Town** – And his name is Simon Leung. When it comes to anything Google, go for the 'Insider Scoop.' Pick up a copy of *Google AdWords Insider* now!"

- Mike Morgan, Million Dollar Copywriter
www.MagicMarketingWords.com

"Thorough, specific, easy to understand. *Google AdWords Insider* is an **absolute must** for anyone marketing on the Internet."

- David Garfinkel, Author, Advertising Headlines That Make You Rich
www.World-Copywriting-Institute.com/blog

"Many people don't realize just how much of a **Google Insider** Simon Leung really is. Nor do they realize the **wealth of wisdom** Simon quietly walks around with - locked up in his brain. But thanks to *Google AdWords Insider*, now everyone smart enough to grab this book can get inside the mind of Simon - THE Creator of Google AdWords optimization himself!"

- Deborah Micek, New Media Coach
www.Quansite.com

"Pay-Per-Click advertising is the single biggest revolution in customer acquisition since the printing press. Now, fortunes can literally be made overnight by harnessing this powerful paradigm shift... but you'll need an experienced guide if you want to climb the learning curve quickly and avoid the pitfalls along the way. Who better to trust than the **ultimate insider**... someone who actually had a hand in designing the Google AdWords system itself? There is simply **no one on the planet better suited to lead you** through the online jungle to the Pay-Per-Click promise land than Simon Leung."

- Sterling Valentine, Six Figures Coach
www.SterlingValentine.com

"Simon Leung... what can I say? The guy is an **absolute genius**! Besides being the Google Insider and AdWords Optimization Expert, I'm happy to know Simon personally. In addition to learning from him through his live presentations and training courses, Simon has also personally helped me develop my own cutting edge strategies using Google AdWords and Web 2.0 properties to bring **massive amounts of traffic to my websites**. And now, Simon is sharing many of these strategies in his new book, *Google AdWords Insider*. There is no hype from Simon... **He is the real deal!**"

- Aimee Vo, Sydney, Australia
www.BusinessAttraction.com.au

"Simon Leung is THE Google AdWords expert. *Google AdWords Insider* is the **next best thing to hiring him**. This book is a **must-read** if you want a competitive advantage."

- Mike Young, Esquire, Internet Marketing Lawyer
www.MikeYoungLaw.com

"Simon is the undisputed KING of cashing in with Google AdWords. He's a **true insider** who came straight from INSIDE the Google AdWords department! So this guy KNOWS what he's talking about. Which means, if you want to discover the real-world truth about **maximizing your profits and sales** using AdWords then you MUST learn from Simon. He gets my **absolute highest recommendation!**"

- Jason Oman, #1 International Best Selling Author of Conversations with Millionaires
www.JasonOman.com

"Not only has Simon consistently been my **go-to resource** for Pay-Per-Click strategies, but in *Google AdWords Insider*, he also OVERDELIVERS and shares the entire strategy for how to **increase conversions and monetization**. Simon has forgotten more information about traffic strategies and lead conversions through Google Marketing than most so-called experts will ever learn!"

- Kevin Nations, The Ultimate Profit Mentor
www.KevinNations.com

"Far more than a primer on Google AdWords, *Google AdWords Insider* gives every business owner a **cut to the chase guide** on how to have a website the generates significant return for their business. The best part? *Google AdWords Insider* is **super easy to read and understand** and the **action steps are laid out** so you can hand the book to your assistant, say 'get it done by next Tuesday' and know it's possible."

- Alexis Neely, Personal Family Lawyer
www.MartinNeely.com


"As a traveling stage hypnotist, it's hard to find time for my personal life, much less for my Internet Marketing business. And when I met Simon Leung in San Diego and heard him speak on stage and learned about his expertise, I knew that I had to hire him for his services. Even though he created my AdWords marketing campaigns for me, I still never really had the time to learn the strategies on my own, until I picked up a copy of *Google AdWords Insider*. This book is **so easy to read and understand** that I know now exactly how he created and optimized my campaigns, and also that I would be able to **duplicate the results myself** if I needed to, and I won't even need to hypnotize myself to do it!"

- Dr. Scott Lewis, Stage Hypnotist
www.VegasHypnotist.com


"I just obtained my **Masters Degree in Google AdWords**, courtesy of Simon Leung's amazing new book, *Google AdWords Insider*. I knew Simon was an insider at Google - **an important team member** in the company's phenomenal success, but he most certainly knows more than just Google AdWords. He also knows how to put everything you need to know down into easy-to-follow steps that are clearly spelled out so you **never wonder where you are** and can easily follow along.

And he does it all with **intimate insider knowledge**, looking at the entire system from the point of views of both Google AND you, the advertiser. Simon has obviously lived on both sides of this river and you're missing out completely if you don't grab a copy of *Google AdWords Insider*. Then, you'll be armed with all you need to know to confidently dive into the rich river of tightly-targeted leads that await you with Google AdWords advertising."

- Alan R. Bechtold, Author of "Will Work for Fun: 3 Simple Steps for Turning Any Hobby Or Interest Into Cash" and Co-producer and star, The FUNdamental You www.FUNdamentalYou.tv

"Wow! *Google AdWords Insider* is awesome. Simon is not only the **obvious expert** on the subject, he also explains his strategies in a way that they are easy to understand and replicate! In just one sitting, this book can easily **turn any AdWords beginner into an expert**."

- Glen Hopkins, #1 Best-Selling Author of Lucrative List Building www.GlenHopkins.name

"After reading *Google AdWords Insider*, I must say that **I know more NOW than I did before** reading the many ebooks out there for AdWords. There are small but very important points and huge tips in this book that I never knew about before that just gave me my 'Ah Ha' moment with understanding the whole AdWords mystery. This book lays out the knowledge first, then the **steps to building your first profitable campaign**. The content is

**extremely easily understandable** without the hypey or technical words used with other books out there which makes for easier and a more motivational read! This book **made me pull out my laptop and follow along** navigating through the Google AdWords program with ease. I totally recommend this book for any newbie or advanced user out there who wants to know the 'truth' about Google! Who better to teach than the MAN himself, the guy who practically developed it!"

- Toki Tover, San Jose, CA
www.TokiTover.com


"Finally! *Google AdWords Insider* is the missing piece of the puzzle and has been well overdue. It really **clears the fog and demystifies** one of the most powerful traffic generation tools of all time.

I now spend **thousands of dollars** on AdWords every month profitably. But when I was starting out, I BURNED thousands of dollars and a LOT of VALUABLE time trying to figure it out by trial and error. All of which **could have been avoided** if this book was available at that time.

*Google AdWords Insider* is a comprehensive, step-by-step manual that will help anyone **create a profitable campaign from scratch**. I wouldn't trust anyone on writing this book other than Simon Leung, who not only developed the techniques, but also used to train Google employees on these strategies.

When it comes to Google AdWords, **Simon is a Genius**. Don't spend money before reading *Google AdWords Insider*."

- Socrates Socratous, The Lead Generation Mentor
www.SocratesSocratous.com

"Simon, you did a great job with *Google AdWords Insider*! The resources that you give are going to inspire people to shut the book and **immediately take action instead of feeling overwhelmed**! You're also going to really shock people as you **clear up a lot of the popular misconceptions** about Google. People will **heavily profit** from this **info-packed, easy-to-read manual!**"

- Rachel Rofe, Philadelphia, PA
www.DoubleTroubleMarketing.com


"Google AdWords is one of the most powerful ways to drive instant traffic to your website. Like many other people, I have found it difficult to really understand how AdWords work and how I could use it effectively.

Then, I finally came across *Google AdWords Insider*, which gives clear step-by-step action plans for everyone who wants to **master AdWords and promote their businesses the right way**. Whether you are just starting with AdWords or an experienced AdWords user searching for new ideas, this book gives huge value and can really take your business to the next level.

Simon Leung has impressive knowledge and wisdom on AdWords thanks to his background in working at Google for many years, and in this book, **he shares it all with you**.

Simon's Google AdWords strategies can work for ANY business, ANY hobby, ANY Idea, ANYWHERE! Congratulations Simon, *Google AdWords Insider* will **help huge number of people in many different industries**."

- Lasse Rouhiainen, Spain
www.LasseTips.com

"*Google AdWords Insider*, the latest book from Simon Leung, has really helped me to get on my Internet marketing game. This book has given me not just the understanding of how important AdWords is in building my business strategically by attracting my targeted best clients, but how to actually do it! From thinking strategically to actual concept to keyword research to writing my ad to setting up my AdWords account and campaigns... **it's all in just this one book** - AND in plain English! I get it now! For any internet marketing entrepreneur, *Google AdWords Insider* **is a must.**"

- Lynn Scheurell, Creative Catalyst
www.MyCreativeCatalyst.com

"I wanted to take a moment to let you know that I have been terrified to run a Google AdWords campaign ever since I started online. This fear has only gotten worse since all this slapping has been going on. Needless to say, I've never run an AdWords campaign before and really haven't taken the time to learn about it because I didn't want to lose my wallet in the process.

All that has changed now since reading your incredibly detailed book, *Google AdWords Insider*. You have **taken me by the hand and led me step by step** through the entire process. I never imagined that it could be this easy.

What I really appreciate is that you go above and beyond teaching me **everything there is to know about setting up and running an effective AdWords campaign**. You taught me the **essential skills which are crucial to achieve the maximum results** from my efforts.

No longer do I fear AdWords. Thanks Simon!"

- Scott Tousignant, The Fit Bastard
www.UnstoppableFatLoss.com

"I met Simon in Hong Kong when both of us were on Christmas vacation. Turns out to me that during that 2 hour lunch meeting with him, **I learnt far more about AdWords than I did watching videos or reading books**. After all, Simon did come fresh from the AdWords oven as a former Google employee. That's the kind of stuff that Simon is made of. I don't say this lightly. Simon's made this book **easy to read, safe to use and very comfortable in the hands of anyone** who doesn't want to keep searching and searching for the diverse amount of information online. This is your **one-stop shop**. Even if you are experienced in using AdWords, you'd probably want this copy for the road. If you're new, don't be surprised at how a complex subject like Google AdWords can be turned into something you can finally practice in the comfort of your own home. Simon, I truly appreciate and admire your dedication to educating everyone on AdWords. I went through this myself, and it makes me wish I hadn't spent the thousands I did on Google related products, and **simply invested in this single product** to help me save money and time. I am looking forward to more great stuff from you!"

- Stuart Tan, Singapore
www.InternetMarketingSingapore.com


"Simon Leung, undisputed king of AdWords experts, shows you **simple ways to leverage the power of Google** to drive massive traffic to your website, grab thousands of new customers and brand yourself and your products to the world -- even if you don't know a thing about AdWords. Simon's **easy system gives maximum impact** for beginners and experts alike!"

- Ken McArthur, Author of "Impact: How to Get Noticed, Motivate Millions and Make a Difference in a Noisy World"
www.TheImpactFactor.com

"*Google AdWords Insider* taught me the **correct usage** of Google AdWords to not only drive massive traffic to my websites, but targeted traffic that actually **converts into sales**! For the Beginners, you will have to read *Google AdWords Insider* to avoid paying "tuition fees" to Google. And for those who are a little more advanced, this book will bring your AdWords campaign to a **whole new level** – just like it did mine!"

- Cassey Lim, Model & Fashion Stylist/Image Consultant
www.CasseyLim.com

"To say it simply, 'Simon is just Awesome!' His sincerity and charm coupled with his accumulated knowledge and practical skills over the years of Corporate and Entrepreneurial Life makes him a very credible mentor, coach, author and platform speaker. In *Google AdWords Insider*, he **reveals the mysteries of Google AdWords from the back stage**. He uncovers the **mind-boggling techniques** into something simple and easy to understand. This book has and will continue to strengthen our 'MAXIMAS Technologies' Online Business Networking Platform ventures, as it help my partners and I gain a deeper understanding on how to use the Internet to our favour. In addition, I'll be keeping it at a bookshelf very near my bed so that I can refer to it once my Purposed Passion book is launched online. Thanks for being such a GEM Simon, I never regret having met you over a year ago in Anaheim and I thank God for letting our paths cross. God bless and may you continue to soar to even greater heights!"

- Jacyln Chan, Marketing Director of Maximas Technologies
www.MaximasNetworking.com

"*Google AdWords Insider* 'spills the beans' about Google AdWords.... and from a guy who actually worked on the inside. Just one glance at the Table of Contents and I knew it was something I HAD to have. The tricks I learned on page 56 and 57 alone will probably mean the **difference to me between a profitable campaign and a failed one.**"

- Frank Sousa, Author and Software Developer
www.ViralCashCow.com

"I am **very impressed** with Simon Leung and his book, *Google AdWords Insider*. I met him during an event that I helped run called The Capital Factor. He gave a 90-minute presentation on AdWords that **shook the audience** in a very positive way.

I, along with many others, took his AdWords course, and was even more impressed. He has a knack for presenting information in an **easy to understand** way, and truly cares about the people he works with.

Thank you Simon for not only **helping me further my career** in Internet Marketing, but for being a great friend."

- Amber Ludwig, Director of The Capital Factor
www.TheCapitalFactor.com

"I just got done reading your new book, *Google AdWords Insider*. I started late, thinking I would read only the first 1/3 but ended up staying up late because **I just could not put it down**. The secrets you tell on Bonus Chapter Four about site targeting and demographic targeting are so powerful that I started to implement them right away. I love this book because it's **simple to read and understand**. Thanks for making something so easy that I feel confident sharing it with anyone!"

- Dan VanOrman, Salt Lake City, UT
www.Media.MyFinishRich.com

"Your new book, *Google AdWords Insider*, is fantastic! Anybody who is spending money on Google AdWords or thinking about testing Google AdWords would be crazy if they didn't **soak up every ounce** of what you teach in this book!"

- Christina Harrison, Terre Haute, IN
www.Rip2It.com

"I am an AdWords professional, I have read just about every book on the subject. However, yours was the only book that covered EVERYTHING. There were a lot of books that were great at basics, a lot of books with powerful advanced techniques, but yours was the **only one that combined them both**.

My wife was able to start learning how to setup my AdWords accounts and then as she made her way through the book...She was even showing me advanced tricks that I had forgotten about. She is an AdWords whiz now thanks to your books.

To anyone reading this...There are a lot of people who teach AdWords. However, do your research on Simon... He is the guy who wrote the training manuals for the first AdWords customer support teams!!!

No one, I mean **NO ONE is more qualified** to teach about Google AdWords than Simon Leung. Simon, I am forever your student!"

- Justin Brooke, Boise, ID
www.MpyreMarketing.com

"The one thing I hear asked all the time by my friends is 'where do I get traffic?' Simon, your book answers that question and takes the mystery out of the most important source of traffic, Google AdWords. *Google AdWords Insider* is **clear and easy to understand**. It helps **overcome the fear of getting started** that many of us have. Thanks, Simon, for bringing your knowledge of AdWords and how it really works to the thousands of small businesses and individuals who **need and will benefit from this information**, myself included."

--Marian Hartsough, Publishing Consultant
www.PublishingAlternatives.com

"*Google AdWords Insider* is a **must have book** for any business wanting to acquire more customers from the most visited search engine on the planet. If you're not using AdWords the way Simon explains it, then you're giving up business to your competition."

- Peter Koning, President, Entra Marketing Ltd.
www.EntraMarketing.com

"At last, a book that **starts at the beginning** and helps a newcomer understand not only how to set up a Google AdWords account, but **how to use it effectively, efficiently, and most importantly, profitably**. True to the title, Simon Leung has made it easy to step through the complicated process of bringing traffic to your website with one of the fastest, most cost-efficient direct response methods ever developed. But if you do it wrong, it can cost you dearly. Which is why *Google AdWords Insider* is a **must-have for anyone who is serious about marketing online**, even if you think you already know AdWords. One tip or technique from this **industry insider** can mean the difference between success and failure. Make it easy on yourself... **read the book**, and take action now!"

- Kathleen Donaghy, Northeast Florida
www.TheArtOfBeingCreative.com

"Finally, a solid book about how to effectively use Google AdWords from an insider who really does know the secrets to AdWords sucess.

Anybody who does any type of e-business has no business using AdWords without reading this first!"

- Brian T. Edmondson, Email Marketing Expert
www.BrianEdmondson.com


"As a former employee at Google, Simon is **uniquely qualified** to share with you how to best Google AdWords to **quickly and consistently generate tons of profits** without breaking the bank. Get *Google AdWords Insider* now and implement this material before your competitors do."

- Alex Nghiem, Atlanta, GA
www.CashNowSecrets.com


"**WOW!!** *Google AdWords Insider* is a **cash-hammer smack to the cranium**!

I'd been fumbling around with AdWords for over two years without ever really getting a solid grasp on it, losing money on the way and about to give up on it altogether. Then I heard Simon Leung was laying everything on the table in his new book and I knew I had to grab a copy!

Right out of the gates Simon over delivers on the meat and potatoes of Google AdWords and gets your pallet ready for a smorgasbord of insider info. I highly recommend tucking a napkin in the collar of your shirt because you may actually salivate while reading this book!"

- Theo Baskind, Spring Hill, FL
www.TheoBaskind.com

"We KNEW after just 5 seconds browsing the *Google AdWords Insider* Table of Contents that this book had **all of the insider-secrets** I needed to start using AdWords correctly, to **explode my business online!**"

Simon is THE **AdWords Guru to the Internet Marketing Gurus** who has that rare ability to show you how to take your ideas and quickly help you implement them for **maximum impact** for your online business growth!

If you are really serious about being a successful Internet marketer – **stop leaving money on the table** and join the 2-5% of us who have followed Simon's recommendations to achieve online financial success!"

- Danny Guspie & Heidi Nabert, The Dynamic Divorce Duo
www.DivorcedDadWeekly.com

"Simon has created a book that is **easy to understand AND follow** and can take anyone to a whole new level on their website. As a "newbie" I will easily be able to start my AdWords campaign and feel confident that I am making wise choices. I expect that with the information I was able to learn from *Google AdWords Insider,* I will easily **increase the amount of traffic to my site and thus increase sales**! Simon also gave other key sites and information to help with researching any topic you might be interested in turning into a website. The best part of the book is that Simon not only tells you HOW to do this, but he actually walks you through the entire process of **optimizing a profitable campaign**. Thank you, Simon, for making your book so easy to understand for even beginners!"

- Tricia Anderson, Brandon, CO
www.AllergyEDU.com

"Simon, you've together an **excellent book on AdWords**. I've read a good few books from people who think they know AdWords – but they don't! You take the reader from the very start all the way to an advanced level. Never before have I really understood how to structure a campaign, or how to increase my quality score for my landing pages – however you've explained this so clearly that anyone can start getting better click thrus at lower prices. If you want to know AdWords, if you want to save money and increase your ROI, take this *Google AdWords Insider* book to the counter now! Don't think just go!"

- Richard Butler, Dublin, Ireland
www.TheSuccessCoach.com

"Great Job, Simon! After reading *Google AdWords Insider*, I have a comprehensive understanding of Google AdWords. **There are golden nuggets for everyone**. Simon created a simplistic easy to read resource guide for the new and seasoned business owner. You unlocked the door to the secrets of how to leverage the power of Google to bring more traffic and cash in the door of ones business."

- Therese Prentice, Social Networking Queen
www.SocialNetworkingQueen.com

"And I thought I knew a thing or two about Google AdWords. Wrong! Simon, your book *Google AdWords Insider* is **THE resource** for advertising with Google. Period. I knew I was onto something when I couldn't put the book down. **You make it all so easy** - from setting up an account to the nitty gritty of actually making AdWords PAY. If anybody wants to use Google AdWords, they had better have this book or they will be left in the dust. Thank you for a terrific resource I know I will use time and again."

- Russell Portwood, Tennessee
www.InternetMarketingToolz.com

"This is not another how-to book on 'writing effective ads'. It is a **step-by-step guide** that will make even the newest of AdWords users feel like a Pro. The strategies revealed uncover everything you need to know about creating and maintaining successful AdWords campaigns **without going broke**. As someone new to PPC, I was thrilled to finally have a book written by the **AdWords Master himself**. Don't create another PPC campaign until you've read *Google AdWords Insider*!"

- Yvonne Lyon, Beverly Hills, FL
www.RevengeOfTheNewbies.com

"Simon's latest book, *Google AdWords Insider*, honestly is one of the most **eye opening books** on AdWords, if not **THE best that I've read** period. There are a ton of resources on how to do AdWords, but Simon pulls back the curtains and take you the reader by the hand on not only what Google AdWords is about, but how to **apply it into your business** from scratch CORRECTLY. By doing so, you are not only able to generate leads, make sales, but you learn a fundamental approach to marketing that is taking the world wide web by storm. It's clear that Simon has mastered this and his willingness to share his knowledge with the general public is truly a gift for us all."

- Geovanni Derice, Author of "Mind Over Matter"
www.Fitness-Success.com

"*Google AdWords Insider* lives up to its name. It is the **definitive soup to nuts guide** for what AdWords is, how to setup a campaign and how AdWords can help you grow your business. Simon does a great job of lifting the veil from Google's cryptic help screens and menu options and walks you through **how to setup a profitable campaign**

**step by step**. If you want to use AdWords profitably, you owe it to yourself to read this book and apply the tips and guidelines in it."

- Rafael Marquez, Austin, TX
www.GoForthSEO.com

"If I had got this book *Google AdWords Insider* earlier, I could have spent less money on my Google AdWords campaigns. I could have also gotten more targeted traffic to my websites. **I strongly recommend you to read this book** IF you are really serious about your business. *Google AdWords Insider* gives you the complete step-by-step fundamental techniques to get around with Google AdWords. Thanks to Simon Leung, the Google AdWords Expert."

- Stephanie Chooi, Malaysia
www.StephanieChooi.com

"Never before has there been a more **complete and easy-to-read guide** than *Google AdWords Insider*! Simon Leung "Demystifies" Google AdWords, making it possible for ANYONE to implement AdWords in an efficient, cost-effective manner. If you are serious about promoting your business online then Simon's books is a **MUST HAVE**. Simon Leung is the undisputed AdWords master without question and his methods will amaze you."

- Gabe Killian, Portland, OR
www.ProfitFromArticles.com

"Simon Leung's *Google AdWords Insider* is an **invaluable resource** for anyone wanting to market their personal brand on the Internet. Simon takes us on an insider's tour of AdWords, turning us all into experts on the details of promotion and marketing."

- Barbara Krvyko, Motivational Speaker
www.BarbaraSpeaks.com

"No wonder I never made any money using AdWords! If only this information had been available to me when I was throwing good money from poor campaigns on AdWords, I wouldn't have stopped using it. Obviously, without this *Google AdWords Insider* information, I was doing about everything wrong you could do and my results proved it. Not only do I now understand what to do and how to do it correctly, **I'm fired up to get a new campaign started**. I'm sorry I wasted so much time and money before I got this book, but I'm grateful I just took the time to read it. This is going to **change my Internet marketing life**! Great job Simon! A million thanks (hopefully, one for every dollar I make!)."

- Pat Hicks, Dallas, TX
www.FreshStartCreditScores.com

"Simon, you wrote a great guide here. I've tried AdWords a few different times and at best had about a 5% ROI, but usually ended up losing money. Your *Google AdWords Insider* book opened my eyes to some of the things that I need to do differently to get things going the way I want them to and **increase my ROI a ton**! Thank you!!!"

- Nick Schultz, Milwaukee, WI
www.ForexInvestingCourse.com

"Whether you're new to the game or have been running your campaigns for some time now, Simon delivers insights into **building a solid AdWords campaign** and teaches you to avoid costly yet common mistakes. *Google AdWords Insider* is a **must read** for everyone who wants to make sure they're getting the best bang for their buck with AdWords!"

- Xurxo Vidal, Co-Founder of Bloom Search Marketing
www.MakeItBloom.com

"I've been marketing online for a few years now and have barely dipped my toe into the AdWords pool. Simon's *Google AdWords Insider* is THE **most comprehensive tutorial I have ever seen**. Don't venture into Google AdWords without it! **Simon is the definitive authority** - why learn this stuff second hand? Thank you Simon - I now feel well equipped to successfully add this valuable resource to my marketing plan."

- Fran Horvath, Prosperity Whisperer
www.ProsperityWhisperer.com

"Very impressive how you take anyone from Google account to AdWords professional! A process that is **as easy to read as it is to implement** with your extensive step-by-step process. Whether you're a "newbie" or "seasoned veteran" you'll find the information in *Google AdWords Insider* to be very informative, and who better to present it to you than a previous Google employee who trained and optimized client campaigns from the inside? **The optimization tips and techniques are priceless**!"

- Joshua Needham, Salt Lake City
www.InternetBusinessProductsExposed.com

"Simon Leung has done it again! You **demystified the Google AdWords realm**, and hey, it's what your book title, *Google AdWords Insider*, told us we were going to get. As a copywriter, some of my clients want Google optimized Namesqueeze pages. Thank you for downloading your knowledge into my brain matrix style so I can let the writing write."

- Matthew Detrick, Direct Response Copywriter
www.MatthewDetrick.com

"Simon, I am at a loss for words! You really should change the name to "The AdWords Bible"! *Google AdWords Insider* is THE **most informative guide to AdWords I have ever read**. The information is simple to understand and is a perfect fit for the newbie or the advanced marketer. You have **outdone yourself again**, and *Google AdWords Insider* will show everyone why you are one of the **leading authorities on Google AdWwords** today. This should be in every marketer's library!"

- Bob Nyce, Scottsdale, AZ
www.CreatingOnlineProfits.com

"If you want to be a Google AdWords authority and do it the best way possible, **learn from Simon Leung**. I had the privilege of hearing Simon speak, I have read his blog, and I will be in line to buy Simon's book. Simon was with Google before they knew what Google was going to be, and has helped many, many people grow their businesses. I have had success with Google AdWords and am building a successful business, and a large part of it is due to Simon Leung and *Google AdWords Insider*. Get this book... because **you should be doing what Simon says**!"

- Kimberly Harrison, Carmel, CA
www.NikaBleu.com

"Finally, Finally, Finally! The book that should only be known as the **"Holy Grail" of Google**. We have intentionally stayed away from Google AdWords because it just sounded difficult! Then our good friend James Lee told us, "Carlos, you have to read my friend Simon Leung, new book, *Google AdWords Insider*." We now know we have lost thousands upon thousands of dollars in lost revenue. If you own a business you need to rush and buy this book now!"

- Carlos and Liz Samaniego, Speakers, Authors and Coaches
www.LizHelpsMoms.com

# Google AdWords Insider

Insider Strategies You Must Master To Instantly
Expose Your Business To 200 Million Google Users

## Simon Leung

**Free Bonus Gifts Online**
Download Exclusive Bonus Chapters,
Reports, Videos, Webinars and More!
GoogleAdWordsInsider.com

**madeeasy**
PUBLISHING

An Imprint of Morgan James Publishing

# Google AdWords Insider

Insider Strategies You Must Master To Instantly Expose
Your Business To 200 Million Google Users

ISBN 978-1-60037-384-8

Library of Congress Control Number: 2010920392

made**easy**
PUBLISHING

An Imprint of:
Morgan James Publishing
1225 Franklin Ave., STE 325
Garden City, NY 11530-1693
Toll Free 800-485-4943
www.MorganJamesPublishing.com

## COPYRIGHT AND TRADEMARK NOTICES

## LIMITS OF LIABILITY & DISCLAIMERS OF WARRANTIES

their correctness, accuracy, reliability, or otherwise. You (and not the Author) assume the entire cost of all necessary servicing, repair or correction. Applicable law may not allow the exclusion of implied warranties, so the above exclusion may not apply to you.

Under no circumstances, including, but not limited to, negligence, shall the Author be liable for any special or consequential damages that result from the use of, or the inability to use the book or the Websites, even if the Author or his authorized representative has been advised of the possibility of such damages. Applicable law may not allow the limitation or exclusion of liability or incidental or consequential damages, so the above limitation or exclusion may not apply to you. In no event shall the Author's total liability to you for all damages, losses, and causes of action (whether in contract, tort, including but not limited to, negligence or otherwise) exceed the amount paid by you, if any, for the book.

Facts and information are believed to be accurate at the time they were placed in the book and on the Websites. Changes may be made at any time without prior notice. All data provided in the book or the Websites is to be used for information purposes only. The information contained within is not intended to provide specific legal, financial or tax advice, or any other advice, whatsoever, for any individual or company and should not be relied upon in that regard. The services described are only offered in jurisdictions where they may be legally offered. Information provided is not all-inclusive, and is limited to information that is made available and such information should not be relied upon as all-inclusive or accurate.

This book and the Websites contain hypertext links to other websites and information created and maintained by other individuals and organizations. These links are only provided for your convenience. The Author does not control or guarantee the accuracy, completeness, relevance, or timeliness of any information or privacy policies posted on these linked websites. You should know that these websites may track visitor viewing habits.

In addition, hyperlinks to particular items do not reflect their importance, and are not an endorsement of the other individuals or organizations sponsoring the websites, the views expressed on the websites, or the products or services offered on the websites.

The Author reviews the book and the Websites periodically for broken or out-of-date links. Any and all links may be posted, altered, or removed at any time. To report problems with links on the website, or for more information about this policy, please contact the Author at the e-mail or mailing address listed in the Copyright Notice for this book.

## EARNINGS AND INCOME DISCLAIMER

### No Earnings Projections, Promises Or Representations

You recognize and agree that the Author has made no implications, warranties, promises, suggestions, projections, representations or guarantees whatsoever to you about future prospects or earnings, or that you will earn any money, with respect to your purchase of this book, and that the Author has not authorized any such projection, promise, or representation by others.

Any earnings or income statements, or any earnings or income examples, are only estimates of what we think you could earn. There is no assurance you will do as well as stated in any examples. If you rely upon any figures provided, you must accept the entire risk of not doing as well as the information provided. This applies whether the earnings or income examples are monetary in nature or pertain to advertising credits which may be earned (whether such credits are convertible to cash or not).

There is no assurance that any prior successes or past results as to earnings or income (whether monetary or advertising credits, whether convertible to cash or not) will apply, nor can any prior successes be used, as an indication of your future success or results from any of the information, content, or strategies. Any and all claims or representations as to income or earnings (whether monetary or advertising credits, whether convertible to cash or not) are not to be considered as "average earnings".

You understand that this book has not been available for purchase long enough to provide an accurate earnings history.

## The Economy

The economy, both where you do business, and on a national and even worldwide scale, creates additional uncertainty and economic risk. An economic recession or depression might negatively affect your results.

## Search Engine Risks

Search engine algorithms run on a unique combination of advanced hardware and software and are not made public. a risk of exclusion from a search engine exists when a search engine views your web site(s) as an unfair manipulation of their service. Many search engine strategies, to improve search engine placement, including the information presented in this book and the Websites may pose such risks.

## Your Success Or Lack Of It

Your success in using the information or strategies provided by this book and at the Websites, depends on a variety of factors. The Author has no way of knowing how well you will do, as he does not know you, your background, your work ethic, your dedication, your motivation, your desire, or your business skills or practices. Therefore, he does not guarantee or imply that you will get rich, that you will do as well, or that you will have any earnings (whether monetary or advertising credits, whether convertible to cash or not), at all.

Internet businesses and earnings derived therefrom, involve unknown risks and are not suitable for everyone. You may not rely on any information presented in the book or on the Websites or otherwise provided by the Author, unless you do so with the knowledge and understanding that you can experience significant losses (including, but not limited to, the loss of any monies paid to purchase this book and/or any monies spent setting up, operating, and/or marketing, and further, that you may have no earnings at all (whether monetary or advertising credits, whether convertible to cash or not).

## Forward-Looking Statements

Materials in this book or at the Websites contain information that includes or is based upon forward-looking statements within the meaning of the securities litigation reform act of 1995. Forward-looking statements give the Author's expectations or forecasts of future events. You can identify these statements by the fact that they do not relate strictly to historical or current facts. They use words such as "anticipate," "estimate," "expect," "project," "intend," "plan," "believe," and other words and terms of similar meaning in connection with a description of potential earnings or financial performance.

Any and all forward looking statements here or on any materials in the book or on the Websites are intended to express an opinion of earnings potential. Many factors will be important in determining your actual results and no guarantees are made that you will achieve results similar to the Author or anybody else, in fact no guarantees are made that you will achieve any results from the Author's ideas and techniques in his materials.

## Due Diligence

You are advised to do your own due diligence when it comes to making business decisions and should use caution and seek the advice of qualified professionals. You should check with your accountant, lawyer, or professional advisor, before acting on this or any information. You may not consider any examples, documents, or other content in this book or on the Websites or otherwise provided by the Author to be the equivalent of legal advice. Nothing contained in this book, on the Websites, or in any other materials available for sale or download on the Websites provides legal advice in any way. You should consult with your own attorney on any legal questions you may have.

The Author assumes no responsibility for any losses or damages resulting from your use of any link, information, or opportunity contained in this book, at the Websites, or within any other information disclosed by him in any form whatsoever.

## Purchase Price

Although the Author believes the price is fair for the value that you receive, you understand and agree that the purchase price for this book has been arbitrarily set by him. This price bears no relationship to objective standards.

## Testimonials & Examples

Testimonials and examples in this book and at the Websites are exceptional results, do not reflect the typical purchaser's experience, don't apply to the average person and are not intended to represent or guarantee that anyone will achieve the same or similar results. Where specific income or earnings (whether monetary or advertising credits, whether convertible to cash or not), figures are used and attributed to a specific individual or business, that individual or business has earned that amount. There is no assurance that you will do as well using the same information or strategies. If you rely on the specific income or earnings figures used, you must accept all the risk of not doing as well. The described experiences are atypical. Your financial results are likely to differ from those described in the testimonials.

You understand that this book has not been available for purchase long enough for the Author to determine what are typical financial results.

# Dedication

*I would like to dedicate this book to my family and friends for the encouragement and support you have given me.*

*A special thanks and acknowledgment of appreciation to the love of my life for being there through everything.*

# Table of Contents

# Foreword By Joel Comm

I met Simon Leung at an Internet marketing conference in the summer of 2006. Even though Simon was still a full-time employee at the time, I instantly sensed the entrepreneurial spirit inside an intelligent young man with an eye on great accomplishments. When I found out his background as the most senior Google AdWords Optimization Specialist at Google's corporate headquarters, I learned that he had already done great things, but he was destined to do much more.

As an authority on Google AdSense, I was thrilled to discover that Simon had worked for Google. In particular, he was a founding member of the Google AdWords Optimization Team, having not only built the infrastructure for the team responsible for managing Google's top advertising clients, but also developing the original optimization strategies used to train internal Google employees around the world.

Today, AdWords is a thriving department within Google that helps advertisers get the biggest bang for their advertising dollar, thanks to the strategies that Simon developed when AdWords was still in its early stages. Without AdWords, there would be no AdSense! You have to have advertisers eager to spend money on clicks in order for publishers to place ads and share in the revenue, which is why we can consider Simon as one of the early pioneers of Internet Marketing who has contributed to the success of many Internet entrepreneurs.

Without a doubt, Google is the current king of online advertising. More corporations, small businesses and individuals spend money to advertise with Google than any other site on the web. The Big "G" rakes in an average of over $10,000,000,000 (That's Ten BILLION) in ad revenue year, with even heftier numbers on the boards for years to come.

That's why it is important for everyone in business to have a rock solid understanding of the AdWords program, and how to leverage Google's network of sites to reach the largest audience possible. After all, if you don't have people visiting your site and/or buying your product online, your Internet business is not going to prosper.

No one knows the Google AdWords contextual advertising system better than Simon Leung. Period.

While Simon left his position with Google after five years, he is still considered the world's leading authority on the subject. While he is not at liberty to divulge any of Google's "confidential" information and trade secrets, the depth of his knowledge and understanding of the topic goes beyond what others know. After all, he has been there and done that. And now, he has written the definitive guide!

You hold in your hands one of the most important books on the topic of online advertising that has ever been written. I encourage you to read this book cover to cover. Highlight key action points. Make sure you implement your AdWords campaign as Simon teaches. And watch your advertising return on investment go through the roof!

To your online success,

Joel Comm
Internet Entrepreneur
www.JoelComm.com

# Introduction And $97 Gift

Google AdWords is considered the fastest and most democratic form of advertising and client generation formula available online. In fact, it all happens at the speed of a mouse click.

A user performs a search on Google, looks to the top or right-hand side of the search results, reads your ad, and clicks on it to visit your website. The visitor instantly lands on your page. And naturally, it is then the job of your website, copy, product or service, offer and overall marketing process to turn your visitors into customers.

Driving traffic to your website is one element of creating a successful Internet Marketing business. When combined with a sales system that works, you have cracked the code to converting your targeted traffic into new business.

Make no mistake – There are countless different ways that people use every day to drive traffic to a website. In fact, these are some of the more traditional strategies that are being taught to maximize exposure for your business.

For example, one of the most popular traffic generation techniques is search engine optimization (SEO), which follows the same process of Google AdWords in that you are getting visits from people who are directly typing in a keyword term into the search engines.

However, while AdWords is considered the paid results on the top and right hand side of the search results page, the organic search results on the left side of the page are considered the natural and "free" results.

Even so, this book is intended to focus completely on creating a Google-Friendly AdWords campaign that works, rather than diving into other aspects of website promotion. Each traffic generation strategy is its own book.

Hence, it is crucial to keep in mind that Google AdWords is not a "magic button," but then, no one marketing element stands alone. That being said, Google AdWords, when implemented correctly and effectively, is the *closet thing* to a "magic button," and for good reason:

### Google AdWords is proven to work for any legitimate business!

It's a fact – Google AdWords is a time-tested system that has been proven to work for thousands of advertisers, whether the end goal is to generate more leads, gain more customers, or test a new idea for a business. Generating qualified leads is traditionally the most challenging aspect for entrepreneurs worldwide. Google

AdWords makes achieving this goal a possibility for any business in record time.

Most businesses have no idea how to even get started with AdWords, which is why since retiring from my Google position in 2006, I have been traveling around the United States and the world, oftentimes flying from city to city and country to country every weekend, to train corporations and small business owners exactly how to use Google AdWords effectively to grow their companies.

In fact, I have expanded my business Internationally with global trainings, creating countless success stories from my clients, students and protégés across the United States, Canada, UK, Singapore, Malaysia, Indonesia, Thailand, Philippines, Hong Kong, China, Australia, and New Zealand, just to name a few.

Interestingly enough, what I have found to be the biggest challenge to most businesses that fail with AdWords is that they simply have no idea what Google wants or how the AdWords system works. Heck, you may even be one of them, and if you happen to be brand new to online advertising, you may even feel intimidated by Google AdWords. With so many mysteries surrounding the AdWords system, it is understandable to wonder whether or not Google AdWords is the right fit for you or your business. Fortunately, you are reading this book.

I have written this book in mind for the complete Internet newcomer, or "newbie" as we like to call Internet neophytes. Even though I will be revealing information about how the AdWords system and review process work from the inside, my intention is to make no assumptions about your knowledge of Google AdWords or Internet Marketing, so this one book is your complete step-by-step guide to getting started and achieving results, even if you currently do not have a product or service to sell.

We are going to start with the research and marketing fundamentals and move on to basic, but effective, optimization techniques that makes the Google AdWords system work. You will need to understand both the concepts of Internet Marketing and Google AdWords to maximize your campaigns.

There are thousands and thousands of pages that can be written about AdWords, but I respect your time and mine, so I am going to cut to the chase by giving you the content straight rather than filling it with fluff. This is because what most people do not know is that all you need to do is master the very basics in order to be successful.

This book is different from all other books on this topic because it gives you all the fundamental strategic elements you need to succeed with Google without going too deep into the technical elements, which often times confuse newcomers and negatively impact their results. Moreover, these are the advanced strategies that are often written, tested and developed by anyone clever enough to trick the system, attaining only temporary successes and resulting in accounts that are penalized, or worse, banned.

In this book, we are only going to focus on the proper fundamentals required to build a Google-Friendly AdWords account, along with the core system elements that will never change. In addition, I have even taken some of the same training modules I developed at Google that are still used today to train brand new Google employees into master AdWords Optimization Specialists. This is the type of information that you will not be able to get anywhere else.

By the time you finish reading this book just one time, I expect you to become, at the very least, an Intermediate level AdWords expert, having created a Google AdWords account with a targeted keyword list and live ads running on Google. Then, as time goes on and you work on further mastering the basics, perhaps even read this book a second, third, fourth and fifth time, you will be well on your way to becoming a Master AdWords Optimizer yourself.

How does that sound to you? Good, I hope. However, you need to remember this one thing to get results: **You need to take action.**

I cannot stress this enough, because if you do nothing, then you will achieve nothing. Many entrepreneurs simply read books and take notes, but never implement the knowledge they have learned, and oftentimes dismissing the information as ineffective without actually doing it. Success comes to those who stop taking notes and start taking action. Make sense?

I am giving you the tools right here to achieve your success. My recommendation is that you read this book from cover to cover. It is now up to you to make that happen. With that said, I wish you the best in your endeavors.

If I can be of further assistance at any time, please do not hesitate to contact me. You can get in touch with me at **GoogleAdWordsInsider.com/support**. Please let me know if you have any questions, and here's to your Google AdWords success!

Thanks,

Simon Leung
SimonLeung.com
GoogleAdWordsInsider.com

P.S. Remember that my goal for this book is to provide you with the "Google AdWords Insider" strategies that you cannot get anywhere else, so I will not waste your time by running through the AdWords account creation process that you can find online.

However, if you feel that you would benefit from an account creation walkthrough, I have created a video that takes you step-by-step through how to create a Google AdWords account the "right" way.

This resource has been selling online as part of a $97 package, but as a surprise bonus, I would like to offer this video as my gift to you. Consider this my way of saying "thank you" for being a reader of my book!

• • • • • • • • • • • • • • • • • • • • • • • • • • • •

Please access your free gift at

**GoogleAdWordsInsider.com/gift**

# Chapter One

# Understanding
# The Google Fundamentals

## *What You Need To Know About Google*

Google has recently emerged as one of the most successful technological companies in history, and it is imperative for your business that you understand Google and Google AdWords as research and marketing tools. We will be taking a closer look at Google not only as a company, but also primarily as a resource that marketers and business owners can use to build their businesses. To grasp the concepts that I will be talking about in this book, you will need to look at Google.com in the way it is perceived online in the Internet world: As a resource.

If you are an absolute beginner and have never even heard of Google.com before, don't worry. This chapter will get you up to speed.

First, what is Google? To Internet users all across the globe, Google is known as "the world's best search engine," but of course, it didn't start there. Founded in 1997 by Stanford University graduates Larry Page and Sergey Brin, Google was a search engine that the co-founders had been working on two years before the business was established.

**Google.com Original Homepage in 1997**

Having originally designed the search engine for Stanford University students, Larry and Sergey worked hard to improve upon the 25 million pages they had indexed at the time. The program was able to handle 10,000 search queries, and the company quickly grew by word-of-mouth alone.

Today, Google has marked its spot as the most dominant search tool on the Web, completely surpassing all competitors with an index of over 25 billion pages, while handing over 200 million search queries every single day.

**Google.com Homepage Today**

In addition to being the leading search engine, Google is also dominating the Internet with its array of other services, including Gmail (web-based e-mail), Google Product Search (online shopping), Blogger (Web logging or blogging service), Google Maps (map and directions), Google Groups (newsgroup), Google News (worldwide news), Google Checkout (payment processing), YouTube (online videos), and dozens more, as listed on their website.

**List of Google Products from Google.com**

Now that Google has basically taken over the online world, you will see a lot more of Google as it invades the world of offline media. You already see Google everywhere on television, but just wait until you see where else Google will end up as it takes on print and radio industries, as well.

Yes, Google has definitely come a long way since its beginnings in a garage what feels like light-years ago in Internet time. It has definitely made its mark in history as one of the fastest growing and most successful technology companies of our time.

## *Why You Must Advertise On Google*

I n February of 2002, Google launched its first Pay-Per-Click (PPC) advertising platform to online advertisers. Known as Google AdWords, the program was a self-service advertising program that provided a way to advertise any business and pay only when the advertising works.

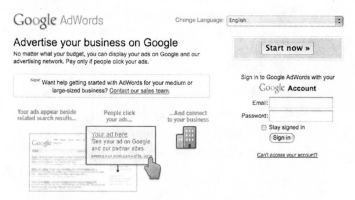

**Google AdWords Homepage at Google.com/adwords**

The concept of Pay-Per-Click means that you, the advertiser, are only charged by the advertising company (i.e., Google) when search users click on your ads. Unlike other advertising programs before this, Pay-Per-Click is not determined by how many times your ad is displayed (impressions). This is especially beneficial to small companies and entrepreneurs because this means that they only pay when they have guaranteed visitors on their websites.

If you have never seen a Google AdWords ad before, open up your browser, go to Google.com, and type a keyword in the search box. The boxed results at the top and along the right side of the search results page, labeled "Sponsored Links," are Google AdWords ads.

**Google Search Results for Keyphrase "simon leung"
– AdWords Ads Appear on the Top and
Right Side of Search Results Page**

Currently, thousands of big and small business owners are advertising on Google AdWords, and with good reasons. First and foremost, Google AdWords works. Thousands of companies are spending millions of dollars advertising on Google because it is giving them the results they are looking for, and it can do the same for you.

With AdWords, you have the potential to harness a tremendous amount of traffic because over 200 million people search on Google every single day to find what they are looking for, and many of these people are looking to buy things. However, that's not all.

Outside of Google.com, Google also has a network of different properties, search partners, content partners, and content publishers that expands its reach to over 80 percent of the users online. This means that if you do not use Google, you are missing out on potentially 80 percent of all Internet users worldwide.

Sample List of Google's Search and Content Partners

In addition, Google has over 25 billion Web pages that are indexed and ready to be viewed by any user who is searching. These same users also have access to 1.3 billion images and one billion sources of user-generated content information, which are messages from forums, chat rooms, bulletin boards, and social networking and community websites.

AdWords has also made it possible for you to get instant traffic to your website. Your ads can be up and running literally within minutes of signing up for your Google AdWords account and creating your first campaign. This translates into immediate Web traffic to your website.

Yet another benefit to using AdWords is the quality of the targeted traffic it brings. When you create your campaign, you only select the most relevant keywords, ad text, and even the locations and languages of your target market. Therefore, only users who search using your specified keywords, who speak the language you chose, and who reside in the area you targeted, will see your ad, and only those who are interested in what you have to offer will click on that ad.

Finally, AdWords gives you affordable traffic. The only financial element standing between your website and massive, instant, and targeted traffic is the low $5.00 USD setup fee for creating your account. After that, you can literally start getting traffic to your site for pennies on the dollar. In many cases, you can even get a decent amount of traffic to your website for as low as $0.01 per click!

In summary, if you are not advertising on Google, you are missing out on potentially hundreds of millions of potential visitors. They could be arriving to your website like clockwork, and all for just pennies on the dollar. This is why you must promote your website on Google and make your presence known to the world.

## *How AdWords Helps You Achieve Your Goals*

By now, you should have a pretty clear understanding of how Google AdWords can benefit a business. However, I am sure you are interested in learning how AdWords can help you specifically. Simply put, Google AdWords can help you with any advertising goal.

For example, with Google AdWords, you can:

- Generate maximal traffic to your website
- Build a subscriber list for your newsletter
- Target traffic to your website in a particular niche
- Capture leads with phone numbers for phone follow-up
- Get potential customers to download a free trial version of your product
- Sell your product or service on your prospect's first visit
- Brand yourself or your product to the public

If you have not already, take some time to determine which of the aforementioned goals apply to you, if any. Every campaign needs to have an end goal in mind so you can test and track your results effectively and make sure you are making progress with your advertising dollars.

Determining your goal will set your strategy for the most effective way to build out your Google AdWords campaign. Be sure to set yours before moving forward with your campaign creation.

# Chapter Two

# Mastering The Basics
# Of Google AdWords

## *Important Things To Understand*
## *About The AdWords System*

Mastery is doing the basics over and over again. After all, you need to learn to walk before you can run, right?

Well, Google AdWords is the same way. I did not wake up one morning and decided that I would become an AdWords expert. In fact, it took many months working for Google within the AdWords department full-time before reaching the level of expertise I eventually acquired. Especially since my core job was to optimize AdWords accounts for advertisers, I needed to know how to do it perfectly (and it took lots of practice!).

Even on my way to expert status, I repeatedly implemented every basic keyword, ad text, account structure and landing page optimization strategy over and over again. These very same optimization strategies that I ultimately mastered are going to be shared with you shortly.

Before we get into that, there is another set of basics that you should first familiarize yourself with – the basics of how the AdWords system works.

The concept is choosing the keywords (search terms or search segments) that relate directly to your business, and create an ad for users to see. When a user searches on a keyword that you chose, he or she will see your ad in the "Sponsored Links" section of the search results. If the user is interested in what your ad says, he or she will click on it and visit your website. It's that simple!

## *Essential Facts About AdWords Costs*

The topic of cost tends to be the number one concern for most new advertisers who are either just getting started, or thinking about getting started. It is a legitimate concern because, after all, it is their hard-earned money we are talking about.

The quick answer to that is that there is a one-time activation fee of $5.00 USD (or the equivalent of $5.00 USD if you are using foreign currency), and this activation fee applies to all brand new accounts. After that, you can set your budget to as little or as much as you would like.

However, the way to go about this is not to consider your advertising dollars as costs, but rather as investments. You are not spending money like you would on clothes, jewelry, or other luxury items. You are investing in the promotion of your business towards getting a massive amount of targeted traffic instantly and affordably, and you are looking to make a return on investment with your advertising budget.

That is precisely the reason why it is so important for you to know your numbers by tracking and testing your results, which is a management technique that will be covered in a later chapter.

The point is, if you know your numbers, and tracked that, say, for every dollar you invest, you get two dollars, five dollars or ten dollars in return, you will then know whether you have a profitable campaign or not. And if you know that you consistently get a 100 percent or more return for every dollar you put in, you can do it all day long!

When deciding your daily budget, you simply decide the maximum amount you want to spend a day.

Additionally, you decide the maximum amount you are willing to spend per click or per impression (on site-targeted ads, which will be covered later on). You only pay when your ad gets results.

Do not stress out too much about what to bid for your terms. Every keyword in every niche is going to be different, and the bid prices are often fluctuating due to competition and changes in the AdWords system.

It would be your best bet to know your budget, and decide how much you are willing to spend on each click. I recommend that you start low, bidding around 10 cents to 50 cents, and see what position you end up displaying in.

After about 1000 impressions (which is the internal number Google uses to assess your campaign performance), you will have a better idea of what kind of prices you can expect to bid on and compete in the market. Most of the time, you can still compete at very affordable prices, especially if you follow the optimization strategies outlined in this book.

# *Vital Billing Cycle Information You Must Know*

The AdWords billing cycle works automatically in that it charges you every 30 days from the day that you created your account, or when you hit a certain threshold credit limit, whichever comes first.

This threshold limit starts off at $50 (at your local currency rate) when you first open up your account. Once you hit the $50, your credit limit will then be raised to $200, then $350, and then finally at $500.

When you have reached the $500 threshold, it will remain at this amount unless you request a higher threshold by contacting Google AdWords support. From then on, every time you hit your credit limit threshold or 30 days, you will be charged. That will mark the beginning of a new billing cycle, where you will be billed either within 30 days or whenever you hit the $500 threshold mark.

## *Crucial Ad Rank Details*
## *That Will Save You A Fortune*

The rank of your AdWords ad is the position it holds on Google's search results. For example, the very top ad would be position number one, and the last ad on the right hand side of the page would be position number eight (depending on the total number of ads being displayed).

In most Pay-Per-Click programs, the rank of an ad is 100% determined by the highest bidder for the respective keyword phrases. This means that the top ad position is more or less guaranteed to the advertiser who is willing to bid the most.

However, with AdWords, your ranking is not simply determined by bidding the highest maximum cost-per-click. Rather, your ranking is a combination between your bid price and what Google calls your Quality Score, which is measured by the system based on keyword relevancy, ad text relevancy, account structure relevancy, landing page quality and the overall performance of your campaign.

Furthermore, your ad ranking depends on your decision to use the search network or the content network (we will get more into the various network syndication options later on in this book).

In addition, the way that the ranking system works is that you only pay one cent higher than your next closest competitor. For example, let's say that you and a competitor are both competing for the number two position. You are willing to bid as high as $0.50, and enter that as your maximum cost-per-click. Your competitor, on the other hand, is only willing to bid up to $0.35.

Assuming that you also have a higher Quality Score than your competitor, you are now eligible to maintain the number two position. On top of that, you do not need to pay the $0.50 cost-per-click that you had put down for your bid; you only pay $0.36 – one cent higher than your next closest competitor.

With this understanding of the way the AdWords system works, you should not get yourself into a bidding war with another advertiser in an attempt to fight for a certain position in the ad's ranking.

You now know that your ad's ranking is a combination between other elements, such as relevancy, quality and performance. And to achieve higher relevancy, quality and performance, you must follow the optimization strategies outlined in this book.

By spending some time mastering the techniques you have in your hands, your ad can outrank your competitors' ads, and you could still be paying less than what they are paying to display lower than you.

## *Search And Content Network Distinctions You Must Realize*

There are two different ways you can advertise on Google – through the search network and through the content network. Because they are two different platforms, their ads are also ranked differently. Here are some details about how ads are ranked for both search and content.

Ads on Google's search network (which are the ones that show when someone enters a keyword term into the Google Search Engine) are keyword-targeted and are determined by a relationship between maximum cost-per-click (CPC) and Quality Score.

The Quality Score of each ad is calculated by a private equation using a variety of factors, including click-through rate (CTR), relevancy, historical performance, landing page quality, and other relevancy and performance history statistics.

Here is the formula: **Maximum Cost-Per-Click x Quality Score = Ad Rank**

The highest-ranking ad will appear in the first position, the next highest will be in the second position, and so on. As you can see, having a sufficient maximum cost-per-click with a high quality campaign will push your ads to the top.

On the other hand, ads on Google's content network are content-targeted and are evaluated differently. Rather than using the Quality Score formula, content-targeted ads are determined by the following factors:

- The Ad Group's content bids (if enabled)
- The Ad Group's maximum CPC (if content bids are not enabled)
- The ad's historical performance on this website or other related websites

It is important to note that site-targeted campaigns do not use a cost-per-click model, but rather a cost-per-thousand impression model (CPM). This means that you will be charged for every 1000 times your ad is displayed.

And because the Quality Score formula does not apply to site-targeted ads, your ad rank will be determined by the maximum cost-per-thousand impression bid.

## Widespread Lie About
## AdWords You Must Not Fall For

One of the most common myths that is being taught today by some well-known experts states that if you want to improve your organic search engine rankings on Google, or if you want to get your website indexed faster in Google's search results, then all you need to do is sign up for an AdWords account, create a campaign, and your rankings will improve after your ad is up and running.

Not only is this "strategy" being taught on the stage and in information products, but is has also been mentioned in conversations between experts.

Here is the truth. Google AdWords is a unique product and a separate department from the search team within Google altogether. In no way, shape or form do your AdWords ads affect your organic search results and listings.

Even to this day, there are several sources and discussions that claim your organic search results can improve by advertising with AdWords. You may also hear that creating an AdWords account is the sure-fire way of getting your website indexed on Google overnight. Anytime you read or hear something like this, ignore it because it is not true.

Google has even publicly announced this to be untrue, and as a public company, it would be fraudulent for them to publish false information about their business practices and technology.

With that said, I hope you understand that this book covers strategies that are meant to improve your advertising results, and not your organic search listings.

# Chapter Three

# Conducting The Right
# Market Research

---

## *Discover Your Passionate Niche Within*

---

This is where it starts. You do realize that in order to make money with Google AdWords, you need to have something to sell, right?

Ideally, you should already have a fairly good idea about what market you want to tackle in your online business. Perhaps you want to take your offline business online, or maybe you want to start something new.

The great thing about the Internet is that there is no loss of opportunity. Thousands of new entrepreneurs go online every day and look to start an Internet business themselves.

There is enough money in the world for every single person to be a millionaire. What this means for you is that you do not need to force yourself to do something that you do not enjoy just to make a buck.

The Internet is full of business opportunities, and you just need to find the right one for you – one that will make you happy and help you reach your personal and professional goals.

To find your niche, one question you can ask yourself is: *What subject or topic am I passionate about?*

Do you enjoy cars? Or sports? Or toys? Or games?

This should get you thinking about what you would do even if you did not get paid to do it. That kind of business is the best one to have.

Another question that you can ask yourself is: *What am I knowledgeable about?*

Unlike popular belief, knowledge is not power. Implementation of that knowledge is the true power. So if you have knowledge about something, do not let it go to waste by not doing anything with it.

You can teach your knowledge by creating information products like an ebook, home study course, or record it in an audio or video format. You can also train people live and do personal coaching. Or, you can start your own service where you provide assistance to your customers.

Yet another question you can ask yourself is: *What would I enjoy learning more about?*

If you are someone who likes to learn, and are always and consistently learning new things, you can create a business where you are learning all the time.

One popular concept is the "interview an expert" model, where you interview an expert a week or a month or as frequently you want to, and while you are providing value to your customers who are listening to you grill your interviewee, you are also learning and consuming the information at the same time.

Finally, ask yourself this question: *What do people ask my advice about?*

If your friends and family members ask you for advice about anything, they most likely perceive you to be an expert or authority on the topic, and highly respect and value your opinion. With this level of credibility, it only makes sense that you start creating a business out of it, since you are already doing it for free with your family and friends.

You may have had some experiences in your life that have transformed you into an expert in dating, family life, careers, food or something else. Chances are that there are people out there looking for your expertise, and will pay you money to get the advice.

It is important that you ask yourself the aforementioned questions in order to figure out the niche that is right for yourself. This niche needs to be something you are passionate and knowledgeable about because you need to enjoy what you do, and you need to have the expertise behind it to leverage your authority.

## *How To Find A Target Market That Will Beg To Buy From You*

The market research process is a crucial part of your project because you need to find a target audience who will buy from you. Unfortunately, many AdWords advertisers who are just starting out go about their market research the wrong way.

What they do is they first ask themselves what they are interested in creating and promoting. After they come up with the product and it is ready to hit the market, they then go out and try to sell it. Force-feeding your preferred product is not market research.

No matter how good your product is, how great a deal you are offering, and how well you have developed your sales presentation, if there is no market for it, it is not going to sell.

With that said, the obvious first logical step you need to take is to do your market research before coming up with your product. This way, you will know for certain that there is a market for your product, and it will eventually be an easy sale to the very people from whom you collected your information. The advantage of doing your market research first lets you figure out what product to make because the response from your market will do all the work for you!

To begin your market research, go to your favorite search engine and start searching on a topic area of your choice. You should pay special attention to any search results for forums, newsgroups, chat rooms, message boards, bulletin boards and any other online communities where people are having active discussions about your topic. In your research, take note of all the problems that these members are experiencing.

Guess what you just did? If you are an information marketer, you just wrote the recipe for your product. And if your goal is to build an empire in your niche, this information will help you dominate your entire market. That's because now, you are going to go out there and either find the solution to the problem, or create one yourself.

This process will reveal if your product is going to be profitable or not because it tells you if there is demand for it in the marketplace. Also, now you know exactly where your target market hangs out, and once your product is complete, you return and announce your answer to their prayers.

## *Market Research Resources You Cannot Live Without*

To find your online target market, you first need to know what keyword terms your market is searching for. Many times, you will find that the keywords you use will be different from what others use, even though you are looking for the same thing.

You need to keep in mind that there are people from different cultures, backgrounds, ethnicities, education and levels of expertise, because all of these elements can affect what a person types into a search engine.

Now, of course, there is almost no way that any one person can just sit down and come up with all these different keyword variations during a brainstorm session, which is why there are keyword research tools available to assist you.

There are many keyword research tools available in the market. Some are free, some are not. Many are web-based, which means that you can use it by using your Internet browser, but there are also some that need to be downloaded and installed into your computer.

As an AdWords advertiser, you have free access to the Google Keyword Tool. For the purpose of conducting research and seeing what other similar terms people search for, this tool is good enough.

**Keyword Tool**

Use the Keyword Tool to get new keyword ideas. Select an option below to enter a few descriptive words or phrases, or type in your website's URL. Keyword Tool Tips

Important note: We cannot guarantee that these keywords will improve your campaign performance. We reserve the right to disapprove any keywords you add. You are responsible for the keywords you select and for ensuring that your use of the keywords does not violate any applicable laws.

Want more keyword ideas? Try the Search-based Keyword Tool, a new tool that will generate ideas matched to your website.

Results are tailored to English, United States Edit

| How would you like to generate keyword ideas? | Enter one keyword or phrase per line: | Selected Keywords: |
|---|---|---|
| ⊙ Descriptive words or phrases (e.g. green tea) | | To advertise with these keywords on Google, export them in TEXT or CSV format. Click 'Sign up for AdWords' to create your AdWords account, then paste the keywords into your new campaign. |
| ○ Website content (e.g. www.example.com/product?id=74893) | ☑ Use synonyms | |
| | Type the characters you see in the picture below. | No keywords added yet |
| | *nmckn* | + Add your own keywords |
| | Letters are not case-sensitive | |
| | ▸ Filter my results | Sign up for AdWords |
| | Get keyword ideas | |

**Google AdWords Keyword Tool**

When utilizing the Google Keyword Tool, simply type in the most relevant keyword term that comes to mind into the tool, click on "Get Keyword Ideas," and the system will automatically generate additional similar terms that people are searching on, as well as its popularity or the number of times they were searched.

The advantage of using the Google Keyword Tool is that this is the most accurate keyword tool on the market that will tell you the popularity of terms searched on Google.com. Even though Google will keep most of the internal statistical data confidential, the tool currently displays an average estimation of your competition, number of local visitors who searched on those terms on the previous month, and number of global visitors who searched on those terms every month.

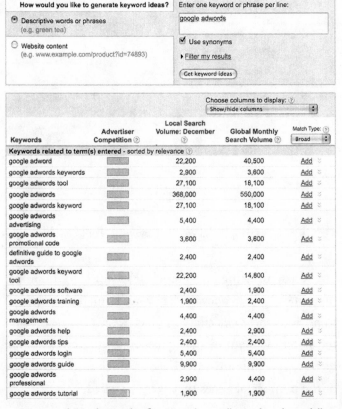

**Keyword Tool Results for Keyphrase "google adwords"**

This information is helpful because you can narrow down your search and refine your keyword terms to the most popular ones, and you can pick and choose which ones you want to use to conduct ongoing research.

Once you have selected the keywords you want to target, you can now proceed in your market research process utilizing one of my all-time favorite tools for any kind of research – Google.com. Remember, over 200 million people use Google every day to find what they are looking for, which includes products, services and information.

If you are not using Google for research purposes, you are missing out on over 25 billion pages of information that you have access to. Since Google is a search engine after all, you can type in the keywords you want that are related to your search, and Google will automatically narrow down the results for you.

But of course, you do not want to stop there. Explore other search engines as well. Some of the more popular search engines include Yahoo.com, MSN.com, Ask.com, Live.com, Excite.com, Lycos.com and AltaVista.com.

Many times, the best results you are going to get will come from forums and other live community based websites because these are the places where people are actively discussing their interests, questions and problems they want to solve.

As mentioned before, take advantage of this opportunity to dive in and find out more about what people are looking for, and quickly turn that around into a product or service that will provide that for them.

When you are ready to dig in a little deeper in your research, you can also begin exploring open markets where there are already products and services available, and you can see how you can contribute to the market and perhaps bring in a completely new concept to improve the current selection.

The way you would do that is by going to a popular online store such as Amazon.com or eBay.com and perform a search on your keyword phrases to see what items come through.

This will give you a better idea on what the market currently has, so you would know not to produce the exact same solution. Always try to distinguish yourself from your competition and make yourself stand out.

## *Key Consideration Points When Determining Your Final Product*

You've done the research. You've found your market. At this point in the game, you should just about be ready to start working on a product or service that will help solve the problems of your prospects.

Believe it or not, this product or service that you are ultimately going to advertise and sell on your landing page can play a big role in how Google determines the quality of your overall campaign. The reason is that Google employees actually visit every website submitted by AdWords advertisers, manually reviewing their content and product or service to make sure that they not only comply with Google's policies, but also that they are considered quality.

This means that you will need to put some work into the creation of your product or service to ensure that it is not only something that your customers can use, but it is also of quality. You can do this by providing an in-depth explanation of your product description that details its quality and what problems it solves. You may also want a high quality image shot of the product or a professional logo so you can give that perception of value.

If you are advertising an offer for a downloadable report or another type of "free" product for your users, make these digital downloads easily accessible to your users. Do not make them jump through hoops in order to get access to them.

Any practices like this would give the perception that you may be a scammer, and that is not the reputation you want to have to your market. Whenever possible, have the resources available for use or direct download straight from your landing page.

Also, your offer should be a solution that your visitor can get through your website. Even with affiliate products, you are still recommending it as the solution to the problem they are looking to solve.

What you should not do is create a "resource page" with links and ads that simply refers them to other links or resources. This type of website is considered poor quality by Google's standards as well as users' expectations.

# Chapter Four

# Designing Google-Friendly Landing Pages

## *Why Google-Friendly Landing Pages Are More Essential Than Ever*

The landing page is the term used to describe the webpage users land on when they click your ad. Within the AdWords system, it is identified as the "Destination URL," and is the main reason that your ad exists in the first place.

Now, more than ever, you are going to have to pay extra attention on how you set up the landing page of your AdWords campaign. For this reason, we must have a strong landing page before you even create your first AdWords campaign, otherwise the quality of your overall account may be negatively impacted.

In case you have not heard about the bombshells Google dropped on their advertisers that those affected have affectionately dubbed the "Google Slap" back in July 2006, many advertisers saw their costs soar and sales dry up because of the apparent low quality of the landing pages on their websites.

Google did this to combat the increasing number of complaints from users about the poor quality of the websites being advertised. To be fair, Google has always had a strong stance in regards to quality. As a matter of fact, Google had been sending the message to all their advertising clients that their AdWords campaign must have high relevance and quality since day one of the AdWords program.

Previous to this development, Google mostly enforced their quality policy on the keywords and ads. However, with the increasing amount of landing pages that contain no content, bad content, and ads offering little to no value to the user, Google was forced to put their foot down on the landing pages as well.

You see, an ad can be perfectly optimized with the most relevant keywords, but the entire experience is useless to the users if they are ultimately taken to a landing page that serves no value to them. People are searching for answers, solutions and information. As an AdWords advertiser, it is your responsibility, obligation and duty to provide that to them.

Google's methods of enforcement surely seem direct and harsh. How is this being enforced, and how would you know if you are being affected? Believe me, you will definitely know if you are indeed affected.

For accounts in which Google determines there is a low Quality Score, the AdWords system will increase the minimum cost-per-click of the keywords in that campaign in order for you to run on those terms. This amount can be $5.00, $10.00, and in some cases, even more.

In order to activate these keywords and be able to run your ads, you will either have to increase your cost-per-click amount to the value specified, or you can increase your Quality Score. If you are like most people, you should opt to increase your Quality Score so that you do not have to pay $5.00 or $10.00 a click!

The good news is that Google provides a public resource that you can follow to improve your Quality Score. Despite being extremely well-hidden inside the Help section on the Google website, these guidelines are still available.

**Landing Page and Site Quality Guidelines**

As part of our commitment to making AdWords as effective an advertising program as possible, we've outlined some site-building guidelines to better serve our users, advertisers, and publishers. We've found that when our advertisers' sites reflect these guidelines, two important things happen:

- This money you spend on AdWords ads will be more likely to turn into paying customers.
- Users develop a trust in the positive experience provided after clicking on AdWords ads (and this turns in to additional targeted leads for you).

Furthermore, following our site guidelines will help improve your landing page quality score. As a component of your keywords' overall Quality Scores, a high landing page quality score can affect your AdWords account in three ways:

- Decrease your keywords' cost-per-clicks (CPCs).
- Increase your keyword-targeted ads' position on the Content Network.
- Improve the chances that your placement-targeted ads will win a position on your targeted placements

Learn more.

Below we've outlined the three main components of a quality website: relevant and original content, transparency, and navigability. Note that these guidelines aren't exhaustive, nor do they replace any of our Editorial Guidelines, which your ads need to comply with in order for you to advertise with AdWords.

Please be aware that there are some types of sites that we've found provide a consistently poor experience for our users. These sites will receive low landing page quality scores. Learn more.

**Relevant and Original Content**

Relevance and originality are two characteristics that define high-quality site content. Here are some pointers on creating content that meets these standards:

**Relevance:**

- Users should be able to easily find what your ad promises.
- Link to the page on your site that provides the most useful information about the product or service in your ad. For instance, direct users to the page where they can buy the advertised product, rather than to a page with a description of several products.

**Originality:**

- Feature unique content that can't be found on another site. This guideline is particularly applicable to resellers whose site is identical or highly similar to another reseller's or the parent company's site, and to affiliates that use the following types of pages:
  - Bridge pages: Pages that act as an intermediary, whose sole purpose is to link or redirect traffic to the parent company
  - Mirror pages: Pages that replicate the look and feel of a parent site; your site should not mirror (be similar or nearly identical in appearance to) your parent company's or any other advertiser's site
- Provide substantial information. If your ad does link to a page consisting mostly of ads or general search results (such as a directory or catalog page), provide additional unique content.

It's especially important to feature original content because AdWords won't show multiple ads directing to identical or similar landing pages at the same time. Learn more about this policy.

**Transparency**

In order to build trust with users, your site should be explicit in three primary areas: the nature of your business, how your site interacts with a visitor's computer, and how you intend to use a visitor's personal information, if you request it. Here are tips on maximizing your site's transparency.

**Your business information:**

- Openly share information about your business. Clearly define what your business is or does.
- Honor the deals and offers you promote in your ad.
- Deliver products and services as promised.
- Only charge users for the products and services that they order and successfully receive.
- Distinguish sponsored links from the rest of your site content.

**Your site's interaction with a visitor's computer:**

- Avoid altering users' browser behavior or settings (such as back button functionality or browser window size) without first getting their permission.
- If your site automatically installs software, be upfront about the installation and allow for easy removal. Refer to Google's Software Principles for more guidelines.

**Visitors' personal information:**

- Unless necessary for the product or service that you're offering, don't request personal information.
- If you do request personal information, provide a privacy policy that discloses how the information will be used.
- Give options to limit the use of a user's personal information, such as the ability to opt out of receiving newsletters.
- Allow users to access your site's content without requiring them to register. Or, provide a preview of what users will get by registering.

**Navigability**

The key to turning visitors into customers is making it easy for users to find what they're looking for. Here's how:

- Provide a short and easy path for users to purchase the product or offer in your ad.
- Avoid excessive use of pop-ups, pop-unders, and other obtrusive elements throughout your site.
- Make sure that your landing page loads quickly. Learn ways to improve your load time.
- Turn to Google's Webmaster Guidelines for more recommendations, which will improve your site's performance in Google's search results as well.

View all related policies.

## Google Landing Page and Site Quality Guidelines

The bad news, as it is even stated on the website, is that this list does not contain hard-and-fast rules, nor is it exhaustive. This means that Google is still trying to determine the criteria that make up a high or low quality site, and these policies are constantly changing and improving.

Furthermore, every website is manually reviewed by a real human, so this adds a level of subjectivity. Likewise, website evaluators could discover new websites they deem to be inappropriate or of low quality. Then, Google may add these website characteristics to their list.

Even with the potentially moving target of quality, there are some surefire strategies to keep in mind when creating your landing page. These are the basics of what Google considers to be quality, and one of the few core elements that will never change in the AdWords system.

## *Exact Types Of Quality Content Google Is Looking For*

When it all comes down to it, Google wants your landing page to be relevant to the product or service that you are advertising in your AdWords campaign. Always think in terms of the user. If you were a user who is searching for something on Google, and you run across an AdWords ad, wouldn't you want to be able to find what you are looking for right when you visit the website?

This is often one of the biggest mistakes advertisers make. When they enter in their Destination URL, they input the homepage of their website, which more likely than not, does not take users to the most relevant page.

You want to be able to provide the highest level of relevance to your visitors so that they do not need to spend more time on your website navigating through different links just to find what they are looking for. If they need to do that, most visitors would end up leaving out of frustration, and you end up losing the sale.

The best way you can do this is by making sure that you have a separate landing page for each of the products or services that you offer. By having the exact same item advertised as the only item available on that page, you maximize the relevancy of your landing page as well as your chances of a successful conversion.

If you want, you can even go one step further by creating a separate page for each of your keywords, even though they are promoting the exact same item. If you do this, Google will consider your landing page to be a higher quality because you have the relevant keywords within the content of your landing page.

Another thing that Google looks for on your landing page is whether or not you have a substantial amount of valuable information. Remember, users who search on Google typically have a problem, and as the content provider, you have the responsibility to provide the answer.

Whether you are selling a product, service or information, make sure that you have enough content on your landing page to at least convince your visitor that you have the knowledge and expertise to provide the solution to them. If you can get them to at least be satisfied with your information that you are giving away for free, they will be happy to pay you to learn more.

Even though it is important to provide this level of high quality content, these days, it is even more important to have unique content. How important?

Having unique content is so important that it will not only increase your website's quality if you have it, but it can also be heavily penalized if you are determined to have duplicate content!

This means that you need to make every effort possible to ensure that the content you have on your website is not duplicated anywhere else on the Internet. Not only does it need to be a substantial amount of quality content, it also must be unique.

Do not simply copy information from articles or other websites (even with permission) to fill up the space on your own landing page. Google will not hesitate to penalize you if you are found guilty of having duplicate content.

Finally, if you have any kind of sponsored links on your own website, which includes banner, image or text ads of any kind, you must clearly distinguish these ads from the rest of your content.

Google wants to make sure that you are the provider of the quality content. There have been too many complaints from people who are upset that they have clicked on an ad with the hope of finding the answers, only to find a page with more ads to click on.

This would result in an extremely poor user experience for the visitors, and when all is said and done, the ultimate goal of any successful landing page (and Google) is to provide a positive user experience, which will maximize your chances of making the sale.

## Understand The Importance Of Building Customer Relationships

Your relationship with your potential customer begins the moment they arrive on your website. This is your first personal interaction with them outside of the AdWords ad, and should continue the conversation from the ad they clicked on. A website that has ads everywhere is not an environment for building relationships.

Once the visitor clicks on your ad and lands on your website, that is your first and only chance to make a positive impression. While design and overall look and feel is indeed an important factor that I will talk more about shortly, there is another element that is far more crucial: The element of trust.

AdWords has done its job by sending a targeted prospect to your website, and now it is your job to earn the trust and respect of this visitor on your page, starting with making your advertised offer easy to find on your landing page.

Remember, people want to be able to find what they are looking for quickly and easily when they land on your website, so do not give them a series of hoops to jump through before being able to locate it.

Ideally, your advertised product or service should be available right on the landing page, complete with full details and a clear description of the offer, an image of the item and the ability to make the purchase right on that page.

When you first read this, you might make the mistake of overlooking this strategy as obvious. However, people will run an ad offering a free product, and then on the page, they request that the user signs up for a credit card, ISP trial, download a software file, or refer a friend. Google considers this a sort of "cyber bait-and-switch."

If you have any types of promotional discounts or deals that you have advertised on your ad or on the landing page itself, make sure that these offers are honored when the customer checks out.

And of course, it goes without saying that once a customer completes the purchase process, you should immediately contact them to confirm the transaction and promptly deliver the product or service as promised.

On your website, you should also have a page where you openly share information about yourself and your company. This can be in an "About Me" or an "About Us" section, where you describe your background and expertise, and why you are qualified to do what you do.

In addition, you want to be completely accessible by your customers if they require support. Include an easy-to-find link to a "Contact Me" or "Contact Us" section of your website, where you have ways to contact you or your support team through a helpdesk system, email, phone and mail.

Doing all of the above will not only improve your credibility to your visitors, but it will also improve your quality with Google.

## *How To Maximize Your Return On Every Click*

Did you know that for most websites, the average conversion rate is between one to three percent? This means that for every 100 visitors who come to your website, 97 to 99 of them end up leaving without buying from you.

Furthermore, a visitor makes that decision whether or not they are going to stay on your website within just eight seconds. On top of that, as many as 50% of these users leave the website immediately after just a glance.

If you are paying money for these visitors to come to your website, that is a large portion of your advertising dollars going straight out the window. Even though most businesses are still making money because of the low cost of their AdWords campaigns, it is still a lot of wasted clicks from people you will never see again.

This is precisely why you must start capturing the leads on your landing page. Remember the free offers that I talked about before? You want to have a free download offer for your visitors that will provide them something of value, something that they want and need. You can capture your visitors' contact information by adding what is called a "name capture form" or an "opt-in box."

In exchange for this free download, all they need to do is give you their name and email address, and the free download link will be sent to them immediately. The reason you want to capture these visitors is so that you have the opportunity to contact them again.

**The Anatomy Of The Six Figure Rolling Launch**

*How To Stuff Your Bank Account With $102,788 In Cash While Enjoying A Week Long Fun Vacation At Disney World!*

Priority List Notification

Enter Your First Name:

Enter Your Primary Email:

Yes, Si! Sign Me Up For Your Priority List!

Click Here To View My Privacy Policy

**Name and Email Opt-In Box from SimonLeung.com**

On average, it takes about seven follow up emails before someone who did not previously buy from you turns around and decides to make a purchase. If they have simply left with no way for you to contact them, then these visitors are essentially gone forever.

You want the opportunity to continue communication with them, earn their trust and eventually convert them into a buyer (especially if you are paying to have them come to your website in the first place).

Even though this is an extremely effective way of marketing your business, many advertisers who capture their leads have run across issues with Google because there are now regulations around this subject. However, they are reasonable rules and extremely easy to follow.

What Google expects when you capture your visitors' information is simply to state the reason why you are collecting it. You can explain in your content that you are going to send them a download link for a free product, weekly or monthly newsletter with relevant content, or ongoing news and updates in your niche.

It is also important that you disclose exactly how their information will be used. For example, you can tell them that it will only be used for follow-ups, content delivery or weekly updates.

Many people are concerned about their privacy and therefore do not typically openly give out their contact information, but if you allow them to limit the use of their information, such as not being automatically subscribed to other newsletters or the ability to opt out of any and all newsletters at any time, they are more likely to subscribe knowing that their privacy is protected.

To further encourage them to subscribe, you should also list the membership benefits. You can list in bullet points the special deals, free offers or insider access that no one else gets by being a subscriber to your newsletter.

Finally, be sure to treat the information of your subscribers responsibly. Do not sell, trade, rent or barter the contact information. Treat their privacy with respect, and you are on your way to building a lifetime of loyal customers.

## Protect Your Business And Increase Quality With Legal Disclaimers

When you are conducting business online, it is essential that you have the appropriate legal disclaimers on your website to protect yourself and your business from just about any potential claims and lawsuits you can imagine.

---

**ADWORDSOPTIMIZATION.COM WEBSITE TERMS OF USE**

**If You Do Not Agree to the Following Terms of Use, Discontinue Using this Site Immediately!**

The AdWordsOptimization.com Web Site (the "Site") is an online information service provided by BuzzMeIn! Marketing ("AdWordsOptimization.com.com "), subject to your compliance with the terms and conditions set forth below.

PLEASE READ THIS DOCUMENT CAREFULLY BEFORE ACCESSING OR USING THE SITE. BY ACCESSING OR USING THE SITE, YOU AGREE TO BE BOUND BY THE TERMS AND CONDITIONS SET FORTH BELOW. IF YOU DO NOT WISH TO BE BOUND BY THESE TERMS AND CONDITIONS, YOU MAY NOT ACCESS OR USE THE SITE. ADWORDSOPTIMIZATION.COM MAY MODIFY THIS AGREEMENT AT ANY TIME, AND SUCH MODIFICATIONS SHALL BE EFFECTIVE IMMEDIATELY UPON POSTING OF THE MODIFIED AGREEMENT ON THE SITE. YOU AGREE TO REVIEW THE AGREEMENT PERIODICALLY TO BE AWARE OF SUCH MODIFICATIONS AND YOUR CONTINUED ACCESS OR USE OF THE SITE SHALL BE DEEMED YOUR CONCLUSIVE ACCEPTANCE OF THE MODIFIED AGREEMENT.

By using this site, you signify your Assent and Agreement to these Terms of Use. If you do not agree to these Terms of Use, do not use the site.

---

Legal Disclaimer Page from AdWordsOptimization.com

This is Internet Business 101 and should not be taken lightly. And while it makes perfect sense to do it for your own welfare, it is also another crucial element of Google's evaluation of your website.

Primarily, Google is looking to make sure that you have the best interest of their users in mind. Obviously, Google wants you to be respectable to their users and that you are taking care of them because, after all, they referred these visitors to you.

This is why you must have a rock solid Privacy Statement or Anti-SPAM Policy that states exactly how you will and will not use the visitors' information. I understand I just mentioned incorporating this into the content of your website, but you also need it as a separate disclaimer page to make it more official.

Then, when you are asking for the contact information of these visitors, you should have an outgoing link right underneath the subscription box that takes users to your complete Privacy disclaimer.

Many marketers who are currently capturing their leads have brief disclaimer messages, such as "We Hate SPAM As Much As You Do," or "We Respect Your Privacy," or something along those lines.

While these messages do give some users a better piece of mind, they are not as official as a dedicated disclaimer page, and to Google, as well as many other users, a simple message like that is not enough.

Specifically, what Google looks for is a disclaimer, ideally placed right underneath your Opt-In Box, which includes a message similar to this: "Click Here To View My Privacy Policy." This must be a live link that opens up the webpage to your Privacy Policy.

As for all other legal disclaimer pages, including Terms and Conditions, Copyright and Earnings Disclaimers, make sure that they are all linked and accessible from all the pages on your website. A good place to put them would be at the bottom of all your web pages.

**Priority List Notification**

**Enter Your First Name:**

**Enter Your Primary Email:**

Yes, Si! Sign Me Up For Your Priority List!

Click Here To View My Privacy Policy

**Link to Disclaimer Page Beneath Opt-In Box**

With a properly structured disclaimer page, you are not only protecting yourself and yourself legally, but you are boosting your credibility in the eyes of Google and your visitors, which will also in turn increase your conversions.

## *Website Design And Graphics Secrets That Will Blow Your Quality Through The Roof*

You should know by now that when Google evaluates your landing page, it looks for quality and unique content. But did you know that "content" applies to more than just the copy you have on your website?

That's right – Content also applies to your website design. The graphical look and feel of your overall layout also needs to be high quality and unique.

Graphically, the website's design should look professional, perhaps even corporate in style. The graphics, images and logos should also be high quality, preferably designed by a professional graphic designer.

This is because when someone comes to your website, you want it to look attractive to the eyes. In some industries, the quality of the website does not really matter. In fact, many websites that would be considered to be unattractive are some of the most successful ones, making millions of dollars.

However, Google stresses quality on all levels. This means that if you want your website to be considered high quality by Google, then you must play by their rules, which means that your website needs to look good.

On the technical side of things, Google wants to see that your website is easy to navigate through, which means that you should include navigational links or buttons either on the top or side of the page.

According to many Google users, there is nothing more frustrating than not being able to navigate through a website and locate what they are looking for. For this reason, Google wants your website to be easily navigable.

In addition, Google wants to see that you are contributing to the rest of the Internet's content by providing natural, relevant outgoing links throughout your website within the content itself.

This does not mean setting up a dedicated page to list all your favorite websites or resources. Google wants to see that you are incorporating these outgoing links as part of references and referrals within the text of your website.

Finally, if you are selling something on your website, make it easy for your visitor to complete the purchase. Have an obvious shopping cart or message that states, "Click Here To Buy," and leave the mystery out of shopping on your website.

# Chapter Five

# Putting Together Effective Account Structures

## *The Three Essential Levels Of The Account Structure*

When it comes to optimization, your account structure is often one of the most important, yet overlooked, aspects of your overall campaign. Building a strong infrastructure for you campaign is essential in the long-term success of your account, yet it is almost always neglected by advertisers, as well as those who teach on the topic of Google AdWords.

Before you can start your journey to success from the targeted AdWords traffic you will convert on your website, it is important that you understand how your AdWords account is structured.

The following visual represents the different levels of an AdWords account:

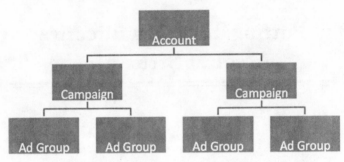

**Account Level, Campaign Levels, Ad Group Levels**

Each level also contains its own components in which certain elements, features and functions are controlled.

### The Account Level

- Unique email address – the email address Google uses to communicate with the account holder.
- User password – the private set of keystrokes you use to be able to access your account from any computer connected to the Internet.
- Customer ID – an internal index used by Google and assigned to your account for reference.
- Billing information – the method of payment on file and the history of your transactions.
- Contact information – a valid email address and phone number where you can be reached.

- Payment options – the methods of payment allowed for AdWords service.

## The Campaign Level

- Campaign name – a user-selected term to help you remember the nature and purpose of your ad campaign
- Start date – the date your campaign will be started by Google.
- End date – the date your campaign ends.
- Daily budget – the maximum daily spending after which no additional ads in the campaign will be served.
- Delivery method – determines how quickly your ads are shown each day. Standard delivery shows your ad over time, while Accelerated delivery shows your ads as quickly as possible.
- Keyword bidding – the ability to set a distinct maximum CPC (cost-per-click) value for certain keywords.
- Ad scheduling – allows you to choose the days and times you want your ads to run.
- Position preference – a feature that will show your ad only when they are to appear in your preferred position or positions indicated.
- Ad serving – determines how the system will serve your ads if you have more than one within the same Ad Group. Optimize automatically displays

the better performing ad the most frequently, while Rotate will display your ads evenly.

- Google search – allows your ad to display when users search on your keyword terms on Google.com.
- Search network – allows your ad to display when users search on your keyword terms in search partner sites within Google's network.
- Content network – allows your ad to display on content partner sites within Google's network, including AdSense publishers.
- Content bids – the ability to set a separate maximum CPC value for clicks generated on sites on the content network.
- Language targeting – the method for selecting a language requirement for your ad to display.
- Location targeting – the method for selecting a geographic requirement for your ad to display.

## The Ad Group Level

- Keywords – the specific search term(s) which will trigger your ad being served (or made visible to the searcher).
- Ad text – the copy or language of the ad that will be served.
- Maximum cost-per-click – your maximum per-click bid.
- Destination URL – the web URL to which the traffic will be sent.

According to published Google resources, a single AdWords account is allowed to have up to 25 campaigns with 100 Ad Groups within each campaign (although you can request additional campaigns from AdWords customer support). Requests are approved if they make sense and are decided on a case-by-case basis.

In addition, there is a 750 keyword per Ad Group limit. However, you cannot have more than 2,000 keywords within a single campaign. The maximum number of keywords the system will allow you to add into your account is 50,000. Google currently has no ad text limitations.

## *Make Life Simpler With An Easy To Navigate Account*

While there are not any hard and fast rules about how you must structure your account, I do recommend that you at least organize your campaigns and Ad Groups by theme, and as specifically as possible.

Now, there are times when your goals may require you to set up your account a certain way (I will talk more about that in the next section). However, in this section, I will go over some ways you can structure your account to make it as easy for you navigate as possible.

The reason you want to create an easily navigable account structure is that you may find that you will need to go back and make changes to your campaigns frequently. And when you do, the account's default settings make it challenging for you to find what you are looking for.

For example, you may notice that when you first set up your account, the first campaign is titled "Campaign #1," and the first Ad Group is titled "Ad Group #1." As you create more campaigns and Ad Groups, the numbers simply increase.

This is why you want to change the campaign and Ad Group names to represent the appropriate theme. Otherwise, as your account grows, it will take you forever and a day to go through your entire account to locate what you are searching.

When it comes to structuring your account, it is most effective if you can categorize them by products and services. For example, one campaign can be dedicated to physical products, where you can sell an ebook in one Ad Group, a published book in a second Ad Group, and a home study course in a third Ad Group.

Then, in another campaign, you can promote services, where you advertise a consultation service in one Ad Group, a full-service program in a second Ad Group, and a coaching program in a third Ad Group.

When you do it this way, you now have control of what promotions are placed in which campaigns and Ad Group. Also, by renaming the campaigns and Ad Groups respectively, you can now easily go through your account and make the appropriate edits should you need to.

If you have different websites or companies that you are promoting, you can also create campaigns based on the domain names. This way, you will know exactly which campaign contains the website that you need to manage.

A great way to obtain new customers is to periodically have promotions, whether they might be for new customers or if they are by season. In this case, you can create Ad Groups that focus on each individual promotion, and you can then go in and turn them on and off as they apply.

Again, there are lots of different ways to set up an account, and there is no single right way. When figuring what works best for you, consider what makes logical sense for your situation, and aim to maximize effective navigation and manageability.

## *Let Your Targeting Decide Your Structure*

When you are first starting out, one of the trickiest things to figure out is how to best structure your account. There are literally dozens of different options, but sometimes, the decision is not necessarily up to you.

One of the first things that will be asked of you is what geographical area you would like to target. You can set your regional targeting preferences, but if you have multiple products that need to be targeted to different locations, these cannot be placed together in the same campaign.

Your regional targeting preferences are set at the campaign level, which means that you cannot have two ads that target different locations within the same campaign. You can, on the other hand, target more than one location (or all countries if you want to) within a single campaign.

For example, if you have an Internet business that offers digital downloads of your product, then you can make sales to anyone in the world. In this case, you would want to create this campaign and target everyone worldwide.

However, let's say that you also have a moving company that services the entire Northern California. You will need to set up a separate campaign that is targeted to individual Northern California cities, such as San Francisco, San Jose, and Sacramento.

Now, let's say that your friend who owns a local pizza parlor in New York also wants to advertise on Google, and you have graciously offered to let him use your AdWords account for this purpose. Since the pizza parlor is local, your friend may want to target only people in New York City, or maybe even only those who are located within a 20-mile radius of the physical address.

In this case, you would need to create yet another campaign to target this pizza parlor. Since your regional targeting preferences are different, you would not be able to target only New York City without targeting the locations in your other campaigns.

Along the same lines, you will need to set up different campaigns if you want to target different languages. Language targeting, much like regional targeting, is set at the campaign level.

This means that if you want to run one ad that targets the English speaking market, and also a second ad that targets the Spanish speaking market, you will need to create two separate campaigns.

On a strategic level, you can also target your campaigns by budget. For example, if you have one product that you would like to spend $100 a day on, and another product that you would be willing to spend up to $1000 a day on, you will need to create two separate campaigns for them because the daily budget is set at the campaign level.

Another targeting feature that AdWords has is Network Targeting, which is the ad syndication functionality that allows your ads to be syndicated across other websites within Google's network. The Google Network reaches out to 80% of all the Internet's users, and includes Google.com and its properties, search network partners and content network partners.

You have the option of opting into more than one of the networks within a single campaign if you wish. However, if you want to syndicate one of your ads and not the other, then you will need to create separate campaigns for them.

# Chapter Six

# Building Powerful Relevant Keyword Lists

## *The Quick And Easy Way Of Doing Keyword Research*

Almost every time I say the phrase "keyword research," people shudder. It sounds like a lot of work, but it really isn't. Don't get me wrong – it is work, but it is quick and easy, and it will be over before you know it.

As mentioned earlier, there are several keyword research tools available on the market. My personal favorite is the one provided free of charge by Google. To start doing your keyword research, simply type in a term or phrase that best describes your product or service into the tool of your choice, and click on the submit button to see what terms might generate.

For example, let's say you are selling an AdWords ebook. This ebook would contain tips and tricks about maximizing your results with Google AdWords.

The keyword research tool may generate the following terms:

## Keywords related to term(s)

adwords ebook

google adwords ebook

free adwords ebook

**Google Keyword Tool Results**

Keyword research tools are designed to give you market and keyword ideas by generating keyword lists. These tools produce phrases that contain the words of your search, but oftentimes, additional analysis is required to find the right terms for you.

To find and select the most suitable keywords for your particular product or service, keep in mind the points I am about to discuss in this chapter.

# *AdWords Success Begins With One Crucial Element*

One of the most important keys to success with Google AdWords is keyword relevancy. Keyword relevancy is critical because you only want to serve ads to users who are highly favorable to your website or product.

When you do keyword research, do not make the mistake of adding every generated keyword into your keyword list. Yes, it is a widely taught method, and it is the easy and lazy thing to do, but keep in mind that if you truly want a successful AdWords campaign, keyword relevancy is paramount.

This is because the keyword term qualifies the user as someone who is interested in your product or service. This is your lead, your potential customer. For this reason, we need to make your keywords as relevant as possible.

Re-examine the three keywords mentioned earlier (*adwords ebook, free adwords ebook, google adwords ebook*). Now, let's say that you are setting up a campaign to sell an AdWords ebook. Which of these terms are relevant?

Here they are again:

- ✓ adwords ebook
- ✓ free adwords ebook
- ✓ google adwords ebook

I am selling an AdWords ebook, so all three are relevant, right? If that is your guess, then guess again! Here's why...

You are selling an AdWords ebook, remember? Therefore, while *adwords ebook* and *google adwords ebook* are relevant, *free adwords ebook* is not. Let me explain.

If users are searching for *free adwords ebook*, chances are that they are not looking to buy anything. While the product you are selling is related to an AdWords ebook, someone who is not intending to buy anything is not a quality visitor (i.e., potential customer) to your ebook selling site.

You will frequently find irrelevant keywords for your campaign in your research. If the terms are not relevant to your campaign, do not add them. Many advertisers do, and let me tell you, it is one of the biggest mistakes they can make when creating their campaigns.

Now, let's say you are selling the same AdWords ebook, and during your keyword research, you run across the following keywords that you want to use:

- ✓ google adwords ebook
- ✓ google adwords guide

Or even:

- ✓ adwords optimization tips
- ✓ adwords optimization help

These are all relevant keywords for a Google AdWords ebook.

Now, during your keyword research, you may find other terms that are somewhat related, but not exactly. For example, you may find keywords such as:

- ✓ google adwords consultant
- ✓ adwords optimization services
- ✓ adwords management company

Do not add them to your keyword list. Chances are that users who are searching for these terms will not click on your ad because they are not interested in your product specifically, in this case, an ebook.

And even if they do click on your ad, they will most likely end up leaving your website without making a purchase because you are not offering what they are looking for.

### Grow Your Traffic
### Exponentially With Far Less Effort

Now that you have identified your most relevant terms from the keyword tools, you want to keep expanding on their additional variations because that is the only way that you can guarantee maximum exposure.

The first thing you need to consider when expanding your keyword list is the keywords' synonyms. A great way to pick up these synonyms is simply by using a thesaurus or going online to Thesaurus.com.

When building out your keyword list, you also need to be mindful that Google does not automatically show a keyword's singular or plural variations automatically. If you are a user of other Pay-Per-Click advertising programs, you may be aware that some of them display both variations as a default.

With AdWords, you must manually add both the singular and plural variations of a keyword term in order to guarantee that your ad displays for all of them. This is important in maximizing your exposure, and many advertisers make the mistake of only including the variation that shows up in the keyword tool.

Another factor to consider is that when users are typing in search queries, they may sometimes spell a word incorrectly or have a typo as a result of typing too quickly. You want to be able to capture these misspelled keywords as well by intentionally adding common misspellings of your keywords into your list.

Even after pulling out the stops with the misspelled variations, keyword expansion does not end there. Next, you need to think about how you can multiply out your terms even more.

One way you can do this is simply by brainstorming additional similar terms. Unlike synonyms, you are not necessarily looking for keywords that have the same meanings. These can be different terms that people are using to search to find the same end product.

An example of synonyms would be *adwords expert* and *adwords specialist*. However, when you add similar terms, you may come up with *adwords tips*, *adwords tricks*, *adwords techniques* and *adwords books*.

While the latter set of words are not synonyms, those who are searching on these terms are all good prospects of any AdWords related product.

You can also multiply out your keywords by combining these terms with action oriented words. For example, if your original keyword is *adwords book*, an action oriented variation of this keyword phrase could be *buy adwords book* or *purchase adwords book*.

The use of an action-oriented keyword will generate a lot fewer displays for you, but the relevancy of your target market that searches on them will be high. More likely than not, those who search on Google with such terms and click on your ad will end up buying what you have to offer.

# *Three Essential Ways To Targeting Your Ideal Prospect*

There are three major ways that you can target your prospects with AdWords, and these three methods are known as keyword matching options. Keyword matching options are the different ways you can target your keywords and are separated into three types: broad match, phrase match, and exact match.

Broad match is the default match type, meaning if you do not specifically enter your keywords as phrase or exact match, any time a user enters your keyword(s) in any order and with any number of other keywords, your ad will display.

Consequently, broad match drives the most traffic to a website. For this reason, I would recommend that you use this match type 90% of the time, provided you do the right keyword research and maintain the keywords' relevancy.

For all of your keywords, including the remaining 10% of your campaigns, take a look at the term *adwords optimization* in the following examples:

## 1) The Broad Match

When *adwords optimization* is broad matched, your ad will display when users enter a search with both of the keywords *adwords* and *optimization* in any order, and even if the query includes other terms, such as *optimization for adwords* and *optimization google adwords.*

With broad matching, the keyword is also automatically enrolled in expanded matching. Expanding matching means that Google will display your ad for other relevant terms, variations and synonyms, even if these terms are not included in the keyword list, such as *optimizing google adwords* and *optimize my adwords campaign.*

The benefit of using broad match is that it provides automatic ad-serving flexibility, which results in the maximum amount of ad exposure and, ultimately, the traffic you can get to your site.

With broad matching, however, you need to be extra careful about keyword relevancy and make sure that your terms are targeted enough to your users.

## 2) The Phrase Match

When *adwords optimization* is phrase matched, your ad will only show when users search on the keywords *adwords optimization* in that order.

To enter the term in your campaign as phrase matched, simply put the words in quotes, e.g., *"adwords optimization"*

When put in quotes, the queries *google adwords optimization* and *adwords optimization tips* will generate your ad, but not *optimization of google adwords.*

The benefit of using phrase match is it allows you to better target your keywords, which will result in higher relevancy and better protect you from sloppy keyword research, allowing irrelevant ads to interfere and cost you money.

### 3) The Exact Match

When *adwords optimization* is exact matched, your ad will only show when users search on the keyword *adwords optimization*. This must be typed in exactly. No other variations of this term will trigger your ad.

To set your keyword for exact match, enter the keywords with brackets, e.g., *[adwords optimization]*.

The benefit of using exact match is that it allows you maximum control in displaying your ad. Although this may dramatically lower your traffic, users who search on your exact term have a higher chance of being ideal customers for you.

## *The Power To Eliminate Keyword Irrelevancy Is In Your Hands*

Google gives you the power to eliminate any and all irrelevant keywords from ever triggering your ad. The system makes this possible by allowing you to block your ad from appearing if users use certain words in their search phrases. The keywords you block are called negative keywords.

For example, if you type in the phrase *google adwords* into a keyword tool, you might see some of the following irrelevant results:

**Keywords related to term(s) entered**

google adwords coupon

google adwords promotional code

google adwords login

Google Keyword Tool Results – Irrelevant Terms

To prevent the irrelevant terms from showing, you need to identify the negative keyword in the phrase. For example, in the keyword phrase, *google adwords coupon*, the irrelevant term is *coupon*. To enter *coupon* as your negative keyword, you simply put a minus sign (-) in front of the word, e.g., *–coupon*. Doing so will prevent your ad from displaying for the search google *adwords coupon*.

Naturally, you would not want to run your ad on that search term, not even if your product includes a *coupon*, because the discount coupon is not the product you are primarily promoting.

Other examples are *-promotional code*, *-login*, or even *-free* to avoid that irrelevant keyword phrase we mentioned earlier, *free google adwords ebook*.

To maximize the relevancy of your keywords, negative keywords are advised for every campaign. You have the power to stop irrelevant search results, so you should do it because you improve your campaign's performance and save money by doing so. Moreover, you do not get traffic that does not want to be there.

Here is a tip: After you turn on your campaign, verify that your ad does not show for your negative keywords. You will learn more about testing your campaign later on in this book. For now, remember to make absolutely certain your negative keywords are working (by not displaying the ad when you search them).

Here is another tip: Make sure that all your negative keywords are terms that you do not want to trigger your ad. You definitely would not want your ad to not display for a perfectly legitimate and relevant keyword simply because it was mistakenly added into the negative keyword list.

# Chapter Seven

# Writing Highly Converting Ads In 95 Characters

## *The One And Only Goal You Must Achieve With Your Ad*

Writing your ad text is arguably one of the key aspects of your entire Google AdWords campaign. After all, the ad text is the language and layout of the ad displayed to your users on the results page, and is the only component of your AdWords account that is visible to the user.

Consider these questions about your AdWords account...

- ✓ Can a user see your keyword list?
- ✓ Can a user see your account structure?
- ✓ Can a user see how much you are bidding?

✓ Can a user see how many times your ad has been displayed?

✓ Can a user see how many times your ad has been clicked?

✓ Can a user see your daily budget?

✓ Can a user see the name on your account?

✓ Can a user see your billing information?

✓ Can a user see how long you have been an advertiser?

✓ Can a user see the end date of your campaign?

✓ Can a user see what other campaigns you are running?

The answer to all of these questions is, "No."

Because the ad text is the only public part of your AdWords campaign, it is the most crucial element separating you from your competition. And as the popularity of Google AdWords continues to grow, so will your competition.

At any given time, your ad can be one of eight or more ads appearing on the same page of Google search results. Since you want your ad to get clicked in order to drive that traffic to your website, you will need a good strategy to distinguish your ad from the other seven or more competitors who are appearing on the same page.

As if the pressure of making your ad text stand out is not enough, Google limits you to just 95 characters for your ad: 25 characters for the first line, 35 characters for the second, and 35 characters for the third.

So you might think the question is: "How do you make these 95 characters sell?"

Actually, it is nearly impossible to sell something in 95 characters. Thus, the short answer is: You don't.

If 95 characters of space is all you need in order to convince someone to buy something, there will be no need for the sales letter, and all the copywriters in the world would be out of business.

Much like an ad in the newspaper, or a commercial on television or radio, the objective of the advertisement is to direct your attention to the main source of the sale. In the case of your AdWords ad, your only goal is to get qualified searchers interested in your advertising message.

You want to capture their attention and interest enough so that they will click on your ad. And on your website, that is where the sales message is, so it is now the job of your copy to convert the visitor into a customer.

# *Only Get Your Perfect Prospects To Click On Your Ad*

You have already started your pre-qualification process for a targeted prospect in the keyword stage. The keywords that you selected should be the exact same terms that people who are looking for your product or service are using.

We talked about the importance of keyword relevancy in the previous chapter. While your keyword list does its job by triggering your ad, it is now your ad's responsibility to get the clicks.

Yes, it is true – You can have the best list of the most targeted keywords in the entire world. But ultimately, these keywords can only be as successful as the ad text with which they are associated.

**By combining relevant keywords with relevant ad text, you create an unstoppable formula for increasing the numbers of targeted visitors at your website!**

For example, let's say you are promoting free AdWords optimization tips, and your keyword list includes terms such as:

| Keyword |
| --- |
| adwords optimization |
| adwords optimization tips |
| adwords optimization help |
| adwords optimization advice |

"AdWords Optimization" Related Keywords

Here is an example of a relevant ad text for these terms:

AdWords Optimization Tips
Free Tips, Help and Advice on Your
AdWords Optimization Needs.
AdWordsOptimization.com

Ad Text for "AdWords Optimization" Related Keywords

Look at this ad closely and then read the explanation
of why this is considered relevant ad text. There are

several factors that would give this ad text a high relevancy score:

1. The ad text mirrors the tightly grouped set of keywords, using the term *adwords optimization*.

2. The main keyword phrase, *adwords optimization*, is inserted into the ad title.

3. The main keyword phrase, *adwords optimization*, is repeated again in the body of the ad.

4. The remaining words within the keyword phrases are contained in the ad text, i.e., tips, help and advice.

5. Finally, searchers will notice the relevance quickly because the keyword used in the search will appear in bold where they appear in the ad text.

## *Demand The Attention Of Your Prospects Before Anyone Else Gets The Chance*

A user types in a search on Google, and your ad is one of eight on the right side of the page. How do you capture the attention of this user and hold their interest long enough so that they will click on your ad and visit your website?

Well, think about it. You are at a newspaper stand, or at the cashier line at the grocery store. There are lots of newspapers and magazines all competing for your attention. How do they do it?

The answer is the headline.

In AdWords, the ad title of your ad has the same general concept as the headline of a newspaper, magazine, or a website. Put simply, it must be **compelling, eye-catching and attention grabbing**.

The ad title is the very first part of your ad that people see, so you must do everything you can to make the most out of the 25 characters of space that Google allows you to use to compel people to look at your ad over your competitors'.

One of the easiest ways to capture that attention is to let the prospects know you have what they are looking for. The way you would do that is by inserting the keyword into your ad title.

If someone is searching on a particular keyword phrase, and then they see an ad that has that exact same phrase in the first line of the entire ad, the relevancy is right on the money. This person is very likely to click on your ad because you have proven that you have what he or she is looking for.

In addition to using your keyword phrases in the actual ad title (which display in bold to the searcher), you can apply ad title optimization strategies that will make your ad stand out.

For example, you can ask a question in the ad title. Although the concept of asking a question makes sense, it is still quite an interesting phenomenon – people are drawn into a question and want to know or give the answer, which further increases their curiosity on what the answer might be.

What I have found in my own tests is that the response is up to five times better if you ask the question where the answer is "Yes." For example, you can ask:

- ✓ What Marketing Help?
- ✓ Need Advertising Advice?

If the keyword used to perform the above searches were "marketing help" or "advertising advice," then the answer to these questions would be "Yes." And if you can connect with your prospects right from the start, you have captured their attention!

Another way you can make your ad title stand out is by making a statement. By making such a declaration, you are stating authoritatively that you have what the prospects are looking.

Using the same keywords just mentioned, we can make the following statements:

- ✓ Marketing Help Here
- ✓ Advertising Advice Now

If I were looking for marketing help or advertising advice, an ad with these ad titles are telling me that I do not need to look any further. I am clicking on the ad, and that will be the end of my worries.

Yet another way you can create a compelling ad title is by making your prospects an offer right then and there. For example, if you are offering something for free or at a discount, make it known to your potential customers right away.

In such a competitive market where you are head to head with others fighting for the same ad space, you must be able to stand out. Hence, if you do have a special offer, you need to let people know about it immediately.

- ✓ Cheap Marketing Help
- ✓ Free Advertising Advice

Now, one potential challenge when you are advertising with such broad terms is the possibility of someone not truly understanding the nature of your offer prior to clicking on your ad.

For this reason, you must sum up the specific product or service you are offering to avoid any confusion. Again, you want to be as specific as possible so people will know what kind of offer you have.

   ✓   Marketing Help Service
   ✓   Advertising Advice Book

This way, if you are offering a service, you will only be attracting those who are looking for a service, and not those who are looking for books, courses or any other types of information products (and vice versa).

## *Guarantee Your Prospects' Understanding Of Your Promotions*

In order to target the right audience, you need to make sure that the description of your product or service in your ad text is absolutely apparent. Remember, a confused mind never buys.

And since you only have 95 characters of space, you only have room to promote one product or service. This means that if you have more than one promotion, you need to create that ad in a new campaign or Ad Group.

When you write your ad, you need to be as clear as possible when describing your product or service. One of the first things people wonder about is what kind of product it is and how it is delivered.

Here are several different types of product descriptions you can consider:

- ✓ Digital product
- ✓ Physical product
- ✓ Information product
- ✓ Software product
- ✓ Service product

In addition to the type of product, you can also be more specific in the description, such as a book, ebook, physically shipped home study course, digitally delivered newsletter, or downloadable files.

If you run out of ideas on how to best describe your product or service, many times, you will notice that the best descriptions are already on your website. Take out the best explanations (or test them between several ads), and use them when writing your ad.

This would be especially beneficial to you because if you are using some of the same copy in your ad as they appear on your landing page, Google will increase your relevancy evaluation.

Back to the user's perspective, you want to make sure that they understand what you are promoting. The clearer you can be, the more likely your ad-clicking visitor is the right visitor. You do not want a user who clicked to your website (costing you money) to leave because of a miscommunication within your ad.

## *Aggressive Competition Means You Cannot Be Just Another Number*

According to several credible sources all over the Internet, there are over 200,000 active advertisers competing for ad space every day on Google (at least that is the current "public" answer). Each day, this number increases.

You can be sure that out of every new advertiser who joins, you are going to start getting more and more direct competition within your own niche.

On the bright side, competition has always existed, not only on AdWords, and not only just online. If you look around you, there are competitors in the form of restaurants, fast food joints, grocery stores, clothing lines, banks, cars and all kinds of electronics.

Yet, many of these companies are still in business, and a majority of them are still making lots of money every day. Again, there is plenty of money to be made, and having healthy competition in business is a good thing because it means that there are still tons of opportunity left to make your fortune.

Even so, you must need to be in the position to compete in order to stake your equal share. With AdWords, you can count the number of competitors on any given page with your two hands.

The way that you would compete in this AdWords game is simple: Distinguish yourself from your competition and make your ad stand out. And you would do that by highlighting very specific special offers while using effective promotional languages in your ads.

Simply use special offers or promotional languages that apply to your product or service, particularly if it is something unique and *especially* if no one else would be able to make the same claim or offer the same deal.

Whenever applicable, include a special offer in your ad, such as:

- ✓ award winning
- ✓ discounts
- ✓ free download
- ✓ free shipping
- ✓ huge savings
- ✓ low price guarantee
- ✓ on sale
- ✓ price matching

...just to name a few.

Now, notice that I said "*whenever applicable.*" This is very important. You must really offer the deal that you advertise in the ad text or your ad text will become both irrelevant and infuriating.

False advertisement not only will cost you the cost of a click without a conversion because the user does not find what he or she is searching for, but it is also against Google's policies (not to mention it is extremely unethical).

## *Create Irresistible Call-To-Actions And Make Prospects Do What You Want*

If you are familiar with copywriting, or even with just marketing in general, you undoubtedly understand that a strong call-to-action phrase is essential in achieving results.

This concept is true in print advertisements, commercials, sales letters, email marketing and almost any other promotional message you can think of. Not surprisingly, Google AdWords is no different.

In fact, since you only have 95 characters across three lines of space to get your point across, a clear and specific call-to-action phrase is especially important.

Also, keep in mind that the 95 characters of space is the *maximum*. If you complete a phrase or sentence with only a few extra spaces left, and it is not enough to fill up another word, then those spaces are pretty much forfeited.

You want your call-to-action phrase to be commanding, and you want it to be clear, telling the user exactly what he or she needs to do on your site. This call-to-action phrase needs to be the exact action that your visitors must take in order to constitute as a successful conversion for you.

For example, if you want the user to sign up for the AdWords Optimization newsletter or the AdWords Giveaway website, your call-to-action ads may be:

AdWords Optimization Tips
Sign Up for the 100% Free AdWords
Optimization Newsletter Today!
TheAdWorder.com

Or

Free AdWords Giveaway
Instant Access to AdWords Products.
Register for Free to Download Now!
AdWordsGiveaway.com

Notice that there are strong call-to-action phrases that are clear and relevant to the desired action: *Sign Up, Register.*

Now, if a successful conversion on your end requires a user to purchase something, say, an AdWords Optimization book or AdWords List Building ebook, your call-to-action would look something like this:

AdWords Optimization Book
Amazing New AdWords Optimization
Book Reveals All. Buy Online Today!
GoogleAdWordsInsider.com

Or

AdWords List Building
How to Build Your List with AdWords
Order Now to Learn Insider Secrets!
AdWordsListBuilding.com

In these examples, strong call-to-actions are used once again: *Buy, Order.*

These phrases are specific, and they spell out to the user what exactly needs to be done on the websites. The descriptive and instructional ads set the user's expectations and leave no room for surprises.

# Chapter Eight

# Managing Accounts For Long-Term Profits

## *Set It And Remember It*

Congratulations! You have set up your account, created your campaign and Ad Group, built your keyword list and wrote your ad. Your AdWords campaign is now live, and you are starting to get a little traffic to your website. Now what?

Many people are under the impression that once you have created your Google AdWords campaign, the flood of traffic will start pouring in on auto-pilot right from the get-go and from here-on-out.

While Google AdWords undoubtedly provides a tremendously powerful channel for massive traffic with huge potential of getting results immediately, you also need to understand that it is a little more complicated than just letting it work itself.

You see, Google AdWords is really pretty fast and easy to set up, but unfortunately, it is not a "set it and forget it" system. And quite honestly, you do not want to put it on auto-pilot.

There are many factors that you need to consider in order to upkeep a successful campaign – quality, return on investment, conversion rates and costs, just to name a few.

If you do not keep a close eye on your advertising campaigns, you will not perform anywhere as close as you could be. Or, you may end up paying much more than necessary.

## *There's Always Room For Landing Page Improvement*

If you are a marketer, or if you are aspiring to be one, testing and tweaking landing pages should not be a new concept.

Whether or not you are using Google AdWords to drive traffic to your landing pages, you should always be making little changes every so often to continually improve your website.

Many times, even the smallest changes can be responsible for an exponential growth in traffic and conversions. That is why you should constantly be making these edits so that your website's results continue to improve.

These changes can be subtle changes, such as adding or deleting one or two elements, or making simple word tweaks within the headline or another part of your copy. Or, they can be bigger changes, such as re-arranging the format, or writing completely new copy all together.

Whatever the caliber of the changes may be, the fact of the matter is that you need to continue tweaking your pages so that you can squeeze the most conversions out of it as possible.

Without tweaking and testing, you will never know how much better you can do, and you will never improve it.

## *Do Not Leave Out The Keywords And Ads*

I know you spent a lot of time building your keyword list. But ultimately, you want a keyword list that is not only performing well for you, but also making money for you. Wouldn't this be worth just a little bit more work?

If you notice that certain terms are not profitable to you, you need to delete them and replace them with new ones. And if necessary, it is also okay to admit that you have built an initial keyword list that does not work for you.

Maybe it could have been more targeted, or relevant, or maybe it just was not right for your target market at the time.

Whatever the case, you need to identify these keywords if they are not producing the results that you want, and know that you can always continue to test new terms that will ultimately work for you.

When it comes to your ad text, it should be treated like the copy of your website. Essentially, they are words that have the power to influence the consumers positively or negatively with just small changes.

In an AdWords ad, we talked about what your goal should be – to get the user to your landing page. The things you need to test are not only the strategies we had already discussed earlier in this book, but they may also be the way that you phrase them.

If you see that you are getting a lot of impressions and a satisfactory position on the first page of results, but very few clicks, you know that your ad text needs to be improved.

There are several things that you can test out…

You can try a new ad title, use different attention-grabbing words, make a different offer, have a different call-to-action, or use a different promotional language phrase.

Basically, what you are trying to do here is figure out what makes your market respond. You will not know unless you test.

## *Life's Too Short To Be Paying Google Too Much Money*

As you continue to advertise, and as you start to evaluate your performance, you definitely need to be mindful in your bidding strategies, and realize that you should shift your budgeting goals as necessary.

For example, you may find that you are performing extremely well, and you are willing to spend more on a daily basis on advertising. Or, you may decide that you want to bid a little more for certain keywords in order for them to increase higher in their positioning.

In these cases, you would want to play around with your maximum cost-per-click and daily budgets, and try increasing them little by little to see if the increased investments would be worthwhile to you.

On the other hand, if you are getting tight on budget, and would like to be more conservative in your spending, you can also adjust your maximum cost-per-click and daily budget amounts to lower values.

By doing so, you will give yourself more room to breathe. You can reduce your spending temporarily until you have had the chance to catch up on whatever it is that you need to do.

This is the great thing about Google AdWords. **The cost of your campaign is always within your control.** You can increase or decrease your spending, and even pause and resume your campaign at will.

# Conclusion And Next Steps

Congratulations on making it to the end of this book! I certainly hope that you did not skip or skim through the pages to reach this section, but rather heeded my advice and read every single word in these pages.

If you indeed took my advice, then you already know more than 90 percent of all entrepreneurs, business owners and even AdWords advertisers. In fact, I would go as far as to say that even current or previous Google employees who read this book would pick up at least one good strategy they did not know or implemented before.

Suffice to say, you may currently have in your intellectual possession more knowledge about AdWords optimization strategies than people who are working in the AdWords department at Google Headquarters.

These are the very same people who are responsible for supporting millions of dollars in ad revenue every single day! And by knowing what you know now, what's to stop you from building your own million dollar or even multi-million dollar empire?

The bad news? Up to 95 percent of those who read this book will end up doing nothing. Despite having this golden vault to AdWords success, these people will simply throw this book aside and forget it ever existed.

I encourage you to be the remaining five percent of the readers who take the knowledge gained from this book, and implement the strategies into your existing or upcoming business.

There is so much opportunity on the Internet and whether you are taking your offline company online or starting up a new online business altogether, AdWords will play a major part in your success.

Of course, there is no way you can remember to apply every single strategy talked about in this book. That is why I encourage you to read it a second, third, and fourth time (more as time goes on), so that you can refresh your learning and also pick up new bits and pieces along the way.

At the very least, follow the step-by-step guidelines in the upcoming bonus chapters to create your AdWords account and get your first ad up and running. This book has taken you from the market research and niche discovery aspect of your business all the way through to having your ad live.

Google AdWords is a goldmine of opportunity for anyone who takes advantage of it and spends the necessary time to master the strategies. It simply doesn't make any sense for anyone to just read this and not do anything with it.

However, do keep in mind that at the end of the day, Google AdWords is a traffic generator to your website. It is ultimately the job of your website to convert these visitors into customers.

Use the strategies outlined in this user-friendly workbook to set the appropriate visitor expectations to your website. This will ensure that you maximize your chances of a successful conversion once the visitors know what to expect.

Throughout the days, weeks and months that follow, be sure to keep a close eye on your account performance, as well as your competition and industry.

If you are on top of the latest developments and make the appropriate changes to your account and your website, you will surely increase your bottom line and maximize your return.

Put the strategies you have learned in this book to use, and read this book again when needed. Through mastering the basics and implementation, you too can become a Master AdWords Optimizer and master the art of potentially bringing over 200 million targeted users to your website instantly and affordably with Google AdWords!

# Bonus Chapters

I have a confession to make: There are more chapters to this book. Why are they not included?

***Because my Publisher said I couldn't!***

That's right – the Founder of the company himself told me personally on a call that these bonus chapters, which were originally part of this book that would have made up over 300 pages, are not allowed to be published because they are too controversial!

However, this is information I still want you to have, so I am going to include these bonus chapters as part of a separate resource you can access online. And while I am making bonuses available, I will also include several more surprises you will find on the download page!

Why am I adding extra bonus chapters to this extensive guide?

If you have completed reading all eight chapters of this book, you now possess enough knowledge about Google AdWords to run a profitable campaign. After all, we have covered everything from market research all the way to creating Google-Friendly landing pages, building effective keyword lists and writing effective ads.

But – Remember the goal from the Introduction of this book? To refresh your memory, the goal is for you to have created your very own AdWords account and have at least one ad up and running by the time you complete your reading.

Even though we have covered all the fundamentals on a strategic level, I understand that there are additional elements of need to also contain a step-by-step guide to the actual AdWords account creation process, management strategies and tools, as well as proprietary resources my team and I use every day to run our own campaigns.

That's why I have created these extra bonus chapters, which contain visual illustrations as I take you by the hand and show you exactly how you can create your AdWords account and campaign, all the way through until your first ad goes live.

These bonus chapters work best if you are using them as a guide while you are in front of your computer setting up your account. Of course, you are welcome to read them whether or not you are on your computer, but they are simply more helpful that way because of its instructional manner.

With the basics of AdWords optimization behind you, the account creation and set up process is a piece of cake. And remember, action takers are the ones who succeed in this business.

You took the first step by picking up this book and reading it. Now, take the next step and follow the step-by-step guidelines in these bonus chapters to create your first AdWords campaign the right way.

• • • • • • • • • • • • • • • • • • • • • • • • • • • •

To access the **Google AdWords Insider Bonus Chapters**, along with additional surprise downloads and complete rolodex of resources mentioned throughout this book, please visit:

**GoogleAdWordsInsider.com/bonus**

# Appendix A

# Glossary Of Basic
# Google AdWords Terminology

This section contains the glossary for some of the most commonly used AdWords terminologies mentioned in this book, as well as elsewhere when the topic of Google AdWords is discussed.

Within your account, you may also see some of these phrases in the campaign summary section or reports.

**Ad** – An individual Google ad within an Ad Group.

**Ad Group** – A group of ads within a Campaign that are focused on a set of keyword phrases.

**Campaign** – Defines the daily budget, language, geographic scope and the networks where ads are displayed.

**Click** – When users click on your ad and are sent to your website.

**Content Targeting** – Displaying of ads on non-Google sites through the Google Content Network.

**CPC** – The cost-per-click of a keyword.

**CPM** – The cost-per-thousand impressions of a keyword.

**CTR** – T he click-through-rate of clicks divided by impressions. A CTR greater than 0.5% is considered to be average. A CTR of 2% or better is very good.

**Daily Budget** – The daily spending limit for an entire campaign. When the daily budget limit is reached for the day, ads will stop displaying until the next day.

**Destination URL** – The actual URL of the page that an ad links to. This must be part of the same domain as the one shown in the display URL.

**Display URL** – The URL shown on an ad. This does not have to be the same page URL as the destination URL, but it must represent the linked to site.

**Impressions** – The number of times an ad has displayed based upon either a user's search using a keywords phrase (Search network) or based upon the content found on a page for a site that is part of the Google AdSense program (Content network).

**Keyword** – An individual keyword or keyword phrase assigned to an Ad Group.

**Keyword Matching Options** – There are four different methods for targeting AdWords ads to more precisely match the ads to the intended search keywords.

**Max CPC** – The maximum cost per click that has been bid for a set of keywords. The bid price is one factor that determines the rank position for an ad.

**Networks Where Ads Are Displayed:**

**Search Network** – Ads displayed on Google search results pages.

**Content Network** – Context-driven ads displayed on non-Google sites through the Google AdSense affiliate network.

**Quality Score** – Click-through rate, relevancy, historical performance, landing page quality, and other relevancy and performance history factors. The Quality Score is the other factor that determines the rank position for an ad.

**Status** – The status of individual keyword phrases within an individual ad. It can be Active, Inactive, Paused or Deleted.

# Appendix B

# Additional Resources

If you are interested in obtaining additional information on Google AdWords products and services, as well as extra Internet Marketing related bonuses, please take a look at my primary website.

**SIMONLEUNG.COM | INTERNET MARKETING POWER BLOG**

**What's Happening At SimonLeung.com?**

Follow Me For Real-Time Updates!

The official site of my blog, I give you regular updates on the progress I have made, the places I have been, the people I have met and the accomplishments I have achieved.

Dated back to April of 2004, the very first day I decided to move forward with an Internet Marketing venture, this blog contains valuable entries on the ups and downs of my journey. I note every mistake I made and every jackpot I hit leading up to the point where I could walk away from a senior position at Google.

Also available is an opportunity to receive regular email updates from me:

The "Internet Marketing Power Blog" Newsletter - Regular news and information on the latest and hottest products to hit the market. Find out about them and begin taking advantage of them before anyone else does!

**To get the most updated information on my various websites, products, services, photos and traveling schedule, visit my Internet Marketing Power Blog and register for my marketing newsletter at SimonLeung.com**

**You can also get up-to-the-minute updates from me all around the world by connecting with me on social media sites like Twitter, Facebook, MySpace, YouTube and more at SimonLeung.com/connect**

# About The Author

Simon Leung, known all across the Internet Marketing industry as the "Google Insider," is one of the world's leading experts in Google AdWords and Internet Marketing.

In April of 2002, back when very few people have even heard about Google.com, Simon became one of the very first individuals to join the Google AdWords team.

For several months, he was one of the highest performers in his role as an AdWords Representative, also known as an Editorial Specialist, manually going through thousands upon thousands of ads during any given week, which gave him the opportunity to ramp up on the Google AdWords product at a very early stage in his career.

After mastering the basic skills of Google AdWords, Simon sought his next challenge as an AdWords Email Coordinator, where he once again became one of the highest performers on his team, cranking through an average of over 100 customer emails on a daily basis.

In addition, Simon even managed customer support over the phone and in the Chinese language, even though the official Phone and International Teams had not yet been established at that time.

Finally, in May of 2003, Simon found his niche. For several months, Simon had been very interested in optimizing clients' Google AdWords accounts and often pro-actively sent optimization suggestions over email and phone. At last, an official Optimization Specialist position rolled out, and there was an opportunity to transition into this position full-time.

However, at the time, there was no Optimization Team. There wasn't even any training or real, tested strategies that had been proven to work. As a matter of fact, Simon was only working on optimizations with one other colleague, who was someone who had joined the AdWords Team a few months after him.

Despite the challenges, Simon worked hard not only to optimize accounts and support clients, but also became instrumental in the testing and developing of the very strategies that are proven to work today. In addition to external client support, Simon also wrote most of the optimization training materials for new AdWords and Optimization Team members, many of which are still being used internally at Google to this day.

Since then, in his position with Google, Simon became not only one of the highest performing members of the team, he also became a leading contributor, trainer, mentor and quality reviewer for all his colleagues. He founded most of the projects that have been valuable to both clients and his team, and he became the number one go-to person on the team with optimization quality and strategy questions.

As an Optimization Specialist, Simon was a tremendous resource internally and externally, working with hundreds of advertisers with all types of problems and successfully helping them achieve their advertising goals. Having improved the performances of thousands of accounts, many of which were new campaigns created from scratch, Simon tested and developed countless strategies with his team and knew from the inside what techniques produced results.

In August of 2006, Simon felt that he had exhausted his learning during his employment at Google, and made the decision to resign from the world's best search engine in search of his next challenge.

Within just two weeks after transitioning into a full- time Internet entrepreneur, Simon had already become a:

- Recognized expert among the top Internet Marketing gurus
- Platform speaker at major Internet Marketing seminars
- Contributor in major product launches by big name speakers
- Special guest on high profile teleseminar calls
- JV partner in several new and upcoming projects
- Creator of several more ground-breaking products of his own

And obviously, Simon has only begun to scratch the surface...

There are a ton of Google AdWords advertisers out there who are frustrated with their advertising efforts, and many more who could benefit from services of all types and at all levels. Simon has now dedicated himself to helping such advertisers in a role and with an angle that he could not have possibly been able to do during his Google employment.

Today, Simon is a full-time Internet entrepreneur and Google AdWords consultant, author, speaker, coach and mentor. He is also the author of several ebooks and audio products, with many more similar products on the way. Simon is often an expert guest and speaker at the highest profile Internet Marketing Seminars in the industry.

As Simon's ideas grow, so do his services. Be sure to take a look at his websites and check back often to see how Simon's latest resources can benefit you, and when he might be speaking in a town near you.

# BUY A SHARE OF THE FUTURE IN YOUR COMMUNITY

These certificates make great holiday, graduation and birthday gifts that can be personalized with the recipient's name. The cost of one S.H.A.R.E. or one square foot is $54.17. The personalized certificate is suitable for framing and will state the number of shares purchased and the amount of each share, as well as the recipient's name. The home that you participate in "building" will last for many years and will continue to grow in value.

### Here is a sample SHARE certificate:

HABITAT FOR HUMANITY

THIS CERTIFIES THAT

**YOUR NAME HERE**

HAS INVESTED IN A HOME FOR A DESERVING FAMILY

1985-2005

TWENTY YEARS OF BUILDING FUTURES IN OUR COMMUNITY ONE HOME AT A TIME

1200 SQUARE FOOT HOUSE @ $65,000 = $54.17 PER SQUARE FOOT
This certificate represents a tax deductible donation. It has no cash value.

## YES, I WOULD LIKE TO HELP!

*I support the work that Habitat for Humanity does and I want to be part of the excitement! As a donor, I will receive periodic updates on your construction activities but, more importantly, I know my gift will help a family in our community realize the dream of homeownership.* **I would like to SHARE in your efforts against substandard housing in my community!** *(Please print below)*

PLEASE SEND ME _____ SHARES at $54.17 EACH = $ $_____

*In Honor Of:* _____

*Occasion:* (Circle One)   HOLIDAY   BIRTHDAY   ANNIVERSARY

   *OTHER:* _____

*Address of Recipient:* _____

*Gift From:* _____  *Donor Address:* _____

*Donor Email:* _____

I AM ENCLOSING A CHECK FOR $ $_____ PAYABLE TO HABITAT FOR HUMANITY <u>OR</u> PLEASE CHARGE MY VISA OR MASTERCARD *(CIRCLE ONE)*

Card Number _____ Expiration Date: _____

Name as it appears on Credit Card _____ Charge Amount $ ____._____

Signature _____

Billing Address _____

Telephone # Day _____ Eve _____

PLEASE NOTE: Your contribution is tax-deductible to the fullest extent allowed by law.
**Habitat for Humanity • P.O. Box 1443 • Newport News, VA 23601 • 757-596-5553**
**www.HelpHabitatforHumanity.org**

LaVergne, TN USA
09 June 2010
185567LV00001B/117/P